Table of Contents

Marriage Petition to U.S. Citizen

Marriage Law Petitions prepared by Immigration Law Firm

Brian D. Lerner

BDL
LAW OFFICES OF
BRIAN D. LERNER
A PROFESSIONAL CORPORATION

ATTORNEY DRAFTED IMMIGRATION PETITIONS

By
Brian D. Lerner
Attorney at Law

Disclaimer and Terms of Use:

Effort has been made to ensure that the information in this book is accurate and complete. However, the author and the publisher do not warrant that this particular petition will mirror or be exactly as your situation. There has not been any attorney-client agreement created by the purchase of this petition or application. No legal advice has occurred. The cases, regulations and/or statutes cited may change at any time without notice.

ISBN: 978-1-948774-95-6

INTRODUCTION

There are a multitude of different immigration petitions and applications. They are complex and full of requirements. Obviously, it would be best to hire an immigration attorney to best prepare the petitions and applications. However, this can certainly cost thousands of dollars.

The next best option is to get a sample of the petition written by an experienced immigration attorney. The samples cost a fraction what would be charged by an immigration attorney. However, while the reader has to alter, amend and change the parts of the sample petition to reflect their actual situation, it is a fantastic roadmap for them to use. If the reader has purchased the entire petition or application, they will have real live samples of cover letters, forms, declarations, affidavits and the necessary exhibits to use. The samples come from real cases and the names of those clients have been redacted to protect the privacy of that person or corporation.

These are petitions and applications that have been drafted by an experienced immigration attorney with over 25 years of experience. Get the benefits of that experience without the costs.

About the Law Offices of Brian D. Lerner

The Law Offices of Brian D. Lerner, APC. The law practice consists of Immigration and Nationality Law and everything involved with and regarding immigration which includes citizenship, investment visas, family and employment visas, removal and deportation hearings, appeals, waivers, adjustment, consulate processing and all types of immigration and citizenship matters. Thousands of families have been reunited and/or permitted to stay in the U.S. and/or return to the U.S. because of the successful work of Immigration Brian D. Lerner.

This law offices handles all types of immigration cases including family based and employment based. Immigration issues range from immigration court proceedings to trying to fix what paralegals may have done that was neither correct nor proper. Foreign nationals must have experience lawyers admitted to practice law.

The Law Offices of Brian D. Lerner, APC, handles cases arising from business visas, work permits, Green Cards, non-immigrant visas, deportation, citizenship, appeals and all areas of immigration. The Law Offices of Brian D. Lerner, APC does EB-5 Investor Visas, H-1B Specialty Occupation, L-1 Intracompany Transferee, E-2 Treaty Investor, E-1 Treaty Trader, O-1 Extraordinary Ability among others. Regarding immigrant visas for the Green Card, the firm does PERM and advanced degree PERM, Family Petitions, and Extraordinary Alien Petitions. In addition to affirmative petitions, the Law Firm represents people in people in deportation and removal hearings, including political asylum, withholding of removal, and convention against torture cases.

Brian D. Lerner has been certified as an expert in Immigration & Nationality Law by the California State Bar, Board of Legal Specialization since 2000 and has been re-certified three times. He now passes on his decades of experience by allowing the Reader, Law Schools, Professors and other Immigration Attorneys to purchase sample petitions on every facet of Immigration Law.

About the Marriage Petition

GETTING MARRIED TO a U.S. Citizen or Lawful Permanent Resident? It is not as easy as just showing your marriage certificate. Immigration basically thinks you are lying about the validity of the marriage and are only doing it to get the Green Card. You must show the bona-fides of the marriage and submit sufficient evidence to show why it is a real marriage for love. This sample Marriage Petition is for you. It has everything necessary to give you the best chance possible to get an approval. Just input your own information and use the application as a guide. It has been prepared by an expert Immigration Attorney. Thus, this book will allow you to see a guide of how it is done, prepared and submitted.

SECTION 1:
Cover Letter

Law Offices of Brian D. Lerner

A PROFESSIONAL CORPORATION

CERTIFIED SPECIALIST IN IMMIGRATION AND NATIONALITY LAW
ADMITTED TO THE U.S. SUPREME COURT

LONG BEACH, CALIFORNIA

CARSON, CALIFORNIA

July 23, 2018

U.S. Citizenship and Immigration Services
PO Box 805887
Chicago, IL 60680-4120

Re: Marriage Petition and Adjustment of Status
Petitioner: Daniel Glenn DEUEL
Beneficiary/Applicant: [redacted]

Dear Sir/Madam:

We hereby enclose the following in support of Mrs. [redacted] (hereinafter "the Applicant") application for adjustment of status:

We enclose the following:

<u>TABLE OF FORMS</u>

<u>Forms:</u>	<u>Description:</u>
G-1145	E-Notification of Application/Petition Acceptance;
G-28	Notice of Entry of Appearance as Attorney or Accredited Representative (Petitioner);
G-28	Notice of Entry of Appearance as Attorney or Accredited Representative (Applicant);
I-130	Petition for Alien Relative with $535.00 Filing Fees;
I-130A	Supplemental Information for Spouse Beneficiary;
I-485	Application to Register Permanent Resident or Adjust Status with $1,140.00 Filing Fees;
I-765	Application for Employment Authorization; and
I-864	Affidavit of Support under Section 213A of the Act, the Petitioner; and
I-864	Affidavit of Support under Section 213A of the Act, the Cosponsor.

Enclosed is the $85.00 Fingerprint Fee. We also enclose two (2) passport style photos of Petitioner and the Applicant.

TABLE OF EXHIBITS

Exhibit:	Description:
'1'	Copy of the Birth Certificate of the Petitioner;
'2'	Copy of the Marriage Certificate of the Petitioner and the Applicant;
'3'	Copy of the Joint 2017 Tax Return of the Petitioner and the Applicant and W-2 Form of the Petitioner;
'4'	Copy of the Birth Certificate of the Applicant;
'5'	Copy of the I-94, Passport, and Visa of the Applicant;
'6'	2017 Tax Return and W-2 Form of the Co-Sponsor, Charina Rivera JOHNSON;
'7'	United States Passport of the Co-Sponsor, Charina Rivera JOHNSON;
'8'	Employment Verification Letter and Current Paystubs of the Co-Sponsor, [redacted]
'9'	Letters of Support from Family and Friends of the Petitioner and the Beneficiary; and
'10'	Photos of the Beneficiary and the Petitioner.

I.

APPLICANT IS ELIGIBLE FOR ADJUSTMENT OF STATUS UNDER SECTION 245 OF THE IMMIGRATION AND NATIONALITY ACT.

Pursuant to section 245(a) of the Immigration and Nationality Act, the Attorney General may adjust the status of an alien who was inspected and admitted or paroled into the United States to that of an alien lawfully admitted for permanent residence if:

(1) the alien makes an application for such adjustment,
(2) the alien is eligible to receive an immigrant visa and is admissible to the United States for permanent residence, and
(3) an immigrant visa is immediately available to her at the time her application is filed.

In the present case, Applicant is eligible for adjustment of status because she was inspected and admitted into the United States (Exhibit 5), he is eligible to receive an immigrant visa, he is admissible to the United States and, as an immediate relative/spouse of a United States citizen, an immigrant visa is immediately available to him.

//
//
//
//
//
//
//
//

II.
CONCLUSION.

Based on the foregoing, we respectfully request that the enclosed applications be approved and that Applicant's status be adjusted to that of a lawful permanent resident.

If you should have any questions, please feel free to contact our office at (562) 495-0554.

Sincerely,

Christopher A. Reed
Attorney at Law

SECTION 2:
FORMS

e-Notification of Application/Petition Acceptance

Department of Homeland Security
U.S. Citizenship and Immigration Services

USCIS
Form G-1145

What Is the Purpose of This Form?

Use this form to request an electronic notification (e-Notification) when U.S. Citizenship and Immigration Services accepts your immigration application. This service is available for applications filed at a USCIS Lockbox facility.

General Information

Complete the information below and clip this form to the first page of your application package. You will receive one e-mail and/or text message for each form you are filing.

We will send the e-Notification within 24 hours after we accept your application. Domestic customers will receive an e-mail and/or text message; overseas customers will only receive an e-mail. Undeliverable e-Notifications cannot be resent.

The e-mail or text message will display your receipt number and tell you how to get updated case status information. It will not include any personal information. The e-Notification does not grant any type of status or benefit; rather it is provided as a convenience to customers.

USCIS will also mail you a receipt notice (I-797C), which you will receive within 10 days after your application has been accepted; use this notice as proof of your pending application or petition.

USCIS Privacy Act Statement

AUTHORITIES: The information requested on this form is collected pursuant to section 103(a) of the Immigration and Nationality Act, as amended INA section 101, et seq.

PURPOSE: The primary purpose for providing the information on this form is to request an electronic notification when USCIS accepts immigration form. The information you provide will be used to send you a text and/or email message.

DISCLOSURE: The information you provide is voluntary. However, failure to provide the requested information may prevent USCIS from providing you a text and/or email message receipting your immigration form.

ROUTINE USES: The information provided on this form will be used by and disclosed to DHS personnel and contractors in accordance with approved routine uses, as described in the associated published system of records notices [DHS/USCIS-007 - Benefits Information System and DHS/USCIS-001 - Alien File (A-File) and Central Index System (CIS), which can be found at www.dhs.gov/privacy]. The information may also be made available, as appropriate for law enforcement purposes or in the interest of national security.

Complete this form and clip it on top of the first page of your immigration form(s).

Applicant/Petitioner Full Last Name	Applicant/Petitioner Full First Name	Applicant/Petitioner Full Middle Name
[redacted]	[redacted]	[redacted]

Email Address	Mobile Phone Number (Text Message)
	[redacted]

Notice of Entry of Appearance as Attorney or Accredited Representative

Department of Homeland Security

DHS Form G-28
OMB No. 1615-0105
Expires 03/31/2018

Part 1. Information About Attorney or Accredited Representative

1. USCIS ELIS Account Number (*if any*) ▶

Name and Address of Attorney or Accredited Representative

2.a. Family Name (*Last Name*): Reed
2.b. Given Name (*First Name*): Christopher
2.c. Middle Name: Allan
3.a. Street Number and Name: 3233 E Broadway
3.b. Apt. ☐ Ste. ☐ Flr. ☐
3.c. City or Town: Long Beach
3.d. State: CA 3.e. ZIP Code: 90803
3.f. Province
3.g. Postal Code
3.h. Country: USA
4. Daytime Telephone Number: 5624950534
5. Fax Number: 5626088672
6. E-Mail Address (*if any*): creed@elrimmigration.org
7. Mobile Telephone Number (*if any*)

Part 2. Notice of Appearance as Attorney or Accredited Representative

This appearance relates to immigration matters before (*Select only one box*):

1.a. ☒ USCIS
1.b. List the form numbers: I-130 I-864
2.a. ☐ ICE
2.b. List the specific matter in which appearance is entered
3.a. ☐ CBP
3.b. List the specific matter in which appearance is entered

I enter my appearance as attorney or accredited representative at the request of:

4. Select only one box:
☐ Applicant ☒ Petitioner ☐ Requestor
☐ Respondent (ICE, CBP)

Information About Applicant, Petitioner, Requestor, or Respondent

5.a. Family Name (*Last Name*): [redacted]
5.b. Given Name (*First Name*): [redacted]
5.c. Middle Name: [redacted]
6. Name of Company or Organization (*if applicable*)

Part 2. Notice of Appearance as Attorney or Accredited Representative *(continued)*

Information About Applicant, Petitioner, Requestor, or Respondent (continued)

7. USCIS ELIS Account Number *(if any)*
▶

8. Alien Registration Number (A-Number) or Receipt Number

9. Daytime Telephone Number
3234042220

10. Mobile Telephone Number *(if any)*
3232440444

11. E-Mail Address *(if any)*
dand45679hotmail.com

Mailing Address of Applicant, Petitioner, Requestor, or Respondent

NOTE: Provide the mailing address of the applicant, petitioner, requestor, or respondent. Do not provide the business mailing address of the attorney or accredited representative unless it serves as the safe mailing address on the application, petition, or request being filed with this Form G-28.

12.a. Street Number and Name: 15723 Tetley Street

12.b. Apt. [X] Ste. [ ] Flr. [ ] 5C

12.c. City or Town: Hacienda Heights

12.d. State: CA 12.e. ZIP Code: 91745

12.f. Province:

12.g. Postal Code:

12.h. Country
USA

Part 3. Eligibility Information for Attorney or Accredited Representative

Select all applicable items.

1.a. [X] I am an attorney eligible to practice law in, and a member in good standing of, the bar of the highest courts of the following states, possessions, territories, commonwealths, or the District of Columbia. *(If you need additional space, use Part 6.)*

Licensing Authority
California Supreme Court

1.b. Bar Number *(if applicable)*
235438

1.c. Name of Law Firm
Law Offices of Brian D. Lerner

1.d. I *(choose one)* [X] *am not* [ ] *am*
subject to any order of any court or administrative agency disbarring, suspending, enjoining, restraining, or otherwise restricting me in the practice of law. If you are subject to any orders, explain in the space below. *(If you need additional space, use Part 6.)*

2.a. [ ] I am an accredited representative of the following qualified nonprofit religious, charitable, social service, or similar organization established in the United States, so recognized by the Department of Justice, Board of Immigration Appeals, in accordance with 8 CFR 292.2. Provide the name of the organization and the expiration date of accreditation.

2.b. Name of Recognized Organization

2.c. Date accreditation expires *(mm/dd/yyyy)* ▶

Part 3. Eligibility Information for Attorney or Accredited Representative *(continued)*

3. ☐ I am associated with ______, the attorney or accredited representative of record who previously filed Form G-28 in this case, and my appearance as an attorney or accredited representative is at his or her request.

   NOTE: If you select this item, also complete Item Numbers 1.a. - 1.b. or Item Numbers 2.a. - 2.c. in Part 3. *(whichever is appropriate)*

4.a. ☐ I am a law student or law graduate working under the direct supervision of the attorney or accredited representative of record on this form in accordance with the requirements in 8 CFR 292.1(a)(2)(iv).

4.b. Name of Law Student or Law Graduate

Part 4. Applicant, Petitioner, Requestor, or Respondent Consent to Representation, Contact Information, and Signature

Consent to Representation and Release of Information

1. I have requested the representation of and consented to being represented by the attorney or accredited representative named in Part 1. of this form. According to the Privacy Act of 1974 and DHS policy, I also consent to the disclosure to the named attorney or accredited representative of any record pertaining to me that appears in any system of records of USCIS, ICE or CBP.

When you (the applicant, petitioner, requestor, or respondent) are represented, DHS will send notices to both you and your attorney or accredited representative either through mail or electronic delivery.

DHS will also send the Form I-94, Arrival Departure Record, to you unless you select Item Number 2.a. in Part 4. All secure identity documents and Travel Documents will be sent to you (the applicant, petitioner, requestor, or respondent) at your U.S. mailing address unless you ask us to send your secure identity documents to your attorney of record or accredited representative.

If you do not want to receive original notices or secure identity documents directly, but would rather have such notices and documents sent to your attorney of record or accredited representative, please select **all applicable** boxes below.

2.a. ☒ I request DHS send any notice (including Form I-94) on an application, petition, or request to the U.S. business address of my attorney of record or accredited representative as listed in this form. I understand that I may change this election at any future date through written notice to DHS.

2.b. ☐ I request that DHS send any secure identity document, such as a Permanent Resident Card, Employment Authorization Document, or Travel Document, that I am approved to receive and authorized to possess, to the U.S. business address of my attorney of record or accredited representative as listed in this form or to a designated military or diplomatic address for pickup in a foreign country (if permitted). I consent to having my secure identity document sent to my attorney of record or accredited representative's U.S. business address and understand that I may request, at any future date and through written notice to DHS, that DHS send any secure identity document to me directly.

3.a. Signature of Applicant, Petitioner, Requestor, or Respondent

3.b. Date of Signature (mm/dd/yyyy) ▶ 07/19/15

Part 5. Signature of Attorney or Accredited Representative

I have read and understand the regulations and conditions contained in 8 CFR 103.2 and 292 governing appearances and representation before the Department of Homeland Security. I declare under penalty of perjury under the laws of the United States that the information I have provided on this form is true and correct.

1. Signature of Attorney or Accredited Representative

2. Signature of Law Student or Law Graduate

3. Date of Signature (mm/dd/yyyy) ▶ 7/23/15

Part 6. Additional Information

Use the space provided below to provide additional information pertaining to Part 3., Item Numbers 1.a. - 1.d. or to provide your U.S. business address for purposes of receiving secure identity documents for your client (if your client has consented to your receipt of such documents under Part 4.)

Notice of Entry of Appearance
as Attorney or Accredited Representative

Department of Homeland Security

DHS
Form G-28
OMB No. 1615-0105
Expires 03/31/2018

Part 1. Information About Attorney or Accredited Representative

1. USCIS ELIS Account Number (if any)

Name and Address of Attorney or Accredited Representative

2.a. Family Name (Last Name): Reed
2.b. Given Name (First Name): Christopher
2.c. Middle Name: Allan
3.a. Street Number and Name: 3233 E Broadway
3.b. Apt ☐ Ste ☐ Flr. ☐
3.c. City or Town: Long Beach
3.d. State: CA 3.e. ZIP Code: 90803
3.f. Province
3.g. Postal Code
3.h. Country: USA
4. Daytime Telephone Number: 5624950554
5. Fax Number: 5626068672
6. E-Mail Address (if any): creed@eimmigration.org
7. Mobile Telephone Number (if any)

Part 2. Notice of Appearance as Attorney or Accredited Representative

This appearance relates to immigration matters before (*Select only one box*):

1.a. ☒ USCIS
1.b. List the form numbers: I-130A I-485 I-765
2.a. ☐ ICE
2.b. List the specific matter in which appearance is entered
3.a. ☐ CBP
3.b. List the specific matter in which appearance is entered

I enter my appearance as attorney or accredited representative at the request of:

4. Select only one box
☒ Applicant ☐ Petitioner ☐ Requestor
☐ Respondent (ICE, CBP)

Information About Applicant, Petitioner, Requestor, or Respondent

5.a. Family Name (Last Name): [redacted]
5.b. Given Name (First Name): [redacted]
5.c. Middle Name: [redacted]
6. Name of Company or Organization (if applicable)

Part 2. Notice of Appearance as Attorney or Accredited Representative *(continued)*

Information About Applicant, Petitioner, Requestor, or Respondent (continued)

7. USCIS ELIS Account Number *(if any)*
▶

8. Alien Registration Number (A-Number) or Receipt Number

9. Daytime Telephone Number
3234042220

10. Mobile Telephone Number *(if any)*
3232440444

11. E-Mail Address *(if any)*
dan d4567@hotmail.com

Mailing Address of Applicant, Petitioner, Requestor, or Respondent

NOTE: Provide the mailing address of the applicant, petitioner, requestor, or respondent. Do not provide the business mailing address of the attorney or accredited representative unless it serves as the safe mailing address on the application, petition, or request being filed with this Form G-28.

12.a. Street Number and Name [redacted]

12.b. Apt. [X] Ste. [ ] Flr. [ ] 5C

12.c. City or Town [redacted]

12.d. State CA 12.e. ZIP Code 91745

12.f. Province

12.g. Postal Code

12.h. Country
USA

Part 3. Eligibility Information for Attorney or Accredited Representative

Select all applicable items.

1.a. [X] I am an attorney eligible to practice law in, and a member in good standing of, the bar of the highest courts of the following states, possessions, territories, commonwealths, or the District of Columbia. *(If you need additional space, use Part 6.)*

Licensing Authority
California Supreme Court

1.b. Bar Number *(if applicable)*
235438

1.c. Name of Law Firm
Law Offices of Brian D. Lerner

1.d. I *(choose one)* [X] *am not* [ ] *am*
subject to any order of any court or administrative agency disbarring, suspending, enjoining, restraining, or otherwise restricting me in the practice of law. If you are subject to any orders, explain in the space below. *(If you need additional space, use Part 6.)*

2.a. [ ] I am an accredited representative of the following qualified nonprofit religious, charitable, social service, or similar organization established in the United States, so recognized by the Department of Justice, Board of Immigration Appeals, in accordance with 8 CFR 292.2. Provide the name of the organization and the expiration date of accreditation.

2.b. Name of Recognized Organization

2.c. Date accreditation expires
(mm/dd/yyyy) ▶

Part 3. Eligibility Information for Attorney or Accredited Representative *(continued)*

3. ☐ I am associated with

the attorney or accredited representative of record who previously filed Form G-28 in this case, and my appearance as an attorney or accredited representative is at his or her request.

NOTE: If you select this item, also complete Item Numbers 1.a. - 1.b. or Item Numbers 2.a. - 2.c. in Part 3. *(whichever is appropriate)*

4.a. ☐ I am a law student or law graduate working under the direct supervision of the attorney or accredited representative of record on this form in accordance with the requirements in 8 CFR 292.1(a)(2)(iv).

4.b. Name of Law Student or Law Graduate

Part 4. Applicant, Petitioner, Requestor, or Respondent Consent to Representation, Contact Information, and Signature

Consent to Representation and Release of Information

1. I have requested the representation of and consented to being represented by the attorney or accredited representative named in Part 1. of this form. According to the Privacy Act of 1974 and DHS policy, I also consent to the disclosure to the named attorney or accredited representative of any record pertaining to me that appears in any system of records of USCIS, ICE or CBP.

When you (the applicant, petitioner, requestor, or respondent) are represented, DHS will send notices to both you and your attorney or accredited representative either through mail or electronic delivery.

DHS will also send the Form I-94, Arrival Departure Record, to you unless you select Item Number 2.a. in Part 4. All secure identity documents and Travel Documents will be sent to you (the applicant, petitioner, requestor, or respondent) at your U.S. mailing address unless you ask us to send your secure identity documents to your attorney of record or accredited representative.

If you do not want to receive original notices or secure identity documents directly, but would rather have such notices and documents sent to your attorney of record or accredited representative, please select **all applicable** boxes below:

2.a. ☒ I request DHS send any notice (including Form I-94) on an application, petition, or request to the U.S. business address of my attorney of record or accredited representative as listed in this form. I understand that I may change this election at any future date through written notice to DHS.

2.b. ☐ I request that DHS send any secure identity document, such as a Permanent Resident Card, Employment Authorization Document, or Travel Document, that I am approved to receive and authorized to possess, to the U.S. business address of my attorney of record or accredited representative as listed in this form or to a designated military or diplomatic address for pickup in a foreign country (if permitted). I consent to having my secure identity document sent to my attorney of record or accredited representative's U.S. business address and understand that I may request, at any future date and through written notice to DHS, that DHS send any secure identity document to me directly.

3.a. Signature of Applicant, Petitioner, Requestor, or Respondent

3.b. Date of Signature (mm/dd/yyyy) ▶ 7/14/18

Part 5. Signature of Attorney or Accredited Representative

I have read and understand the regulations and conditions contained in 8 CFR 103.2 and 292 governing appearances and representation before the Department of Homeland Security. I declare under penalty of perjury under the laws of the United States that the information I have provided on this form is true and correct.

1. Signature of Attorney or Accredited Representative

2. Signature of Law Student or Law Graduate

3. Date of Signature (mm/dd/yyyy) ▶ 7/23/18

Part 6. Additional Information

Use the space provided below to provide additional information pertaining to Part 3., Item Numbers 1.a. - 1.d. or to provide your U.S. business address for purposes of receiving secure identity documents for your client (if your client has consented to your receipt of such documents under Part 4.)

Petition for Alien Relative

Department of Homeland Security
U.S. Citizenship and Immigration Services

USCIS
Form I-130
OMB No. 1615-0012
Expires 03/31/2018

For USCIS Use Only	Fee Stamp	Action Stamp
A-Number A-		
Initial Receipt		
Resubmitted		
Relocated	Section of Law/Visa Category	
Received	☐ 201(b) Spouse - IR-1/CR-1 ☐ 203(a)(1) Unm. S/D - F1-1 ☐ 203(a)(2)(B) Unm. S/D - F2-4	
Sent	☐ 201(b) Child - IR-2/CR-2 ☐ 203(a)(2)(A) Spouse - F2-1 ☐ 203(a)(3) Married S/D - F3-1	
Completed	☐ 201(b) Parent - IR-5 ☐ 203(a)(2)(A) Child - F2-2 ☐ 203(a)(4) Brother/Sister - F4-1	
Approved	Petition was filed on (Priority Date mm/dd/yyyy):	☐ Field Investigation ☐ Personal Interview ☐ 204(a)(2)(A) Resolved
Returned	PDR request granted/denied - New priority date (mm/dd/yyyy):	☐ Previously Forwarded ☐ Pet. A-File Reviewed ☐ I-485 Filed Simultaneously ☐ 203(g) Resolved ☐ Ben. A-File Reviewed ☐ 204(g) Resolved
Remarks		

At which USCIS office (e.g., NBC, VSC, LOS, CRO) was Form I-130 adjudicated? ____________

To be completed by an attorney or accredited representative (if any).			
☒ Select this box if Form G-28 is attached.	Volag Number (if any)	Attorney State Bar Number (if applicable)	Attorney or Accredited Representative USCIS Online Account Number (if any)

▶ **START HERE** - Type or print in black ink.

If you need extra space to complete any section of this petition, use the space provided in Part 9. Additional Information. Complete and submit as many copies of Part 9., as necessary, with your petition.

Part 1. Relationship (You are the Petitioner. Your relative is the Beneficiary)

1. I am filing this petition for my (Select only one box):
☒ Spouse ☐ Parent ☐ Brother/Sister ☐ Child

2. If you are filing this petition for your child or parent, select the box that describes your relationship (Select only one box):
☐ Child was born to parents who were married to each other at the time of the child's birth
☐ Stepchild/Stepparent
☐ Child was born to parents who were not married to each other at the time of the child's birth
☐ Child was adopted (not an Orphan or Hague Convention adoptee)

3. If the beneficiary is your brother/sister, are you related by adoption? ☐ Yes ☒ No

4. Did you gain lawful permanent resident status or citizenship through adoption? ☐ Yes ☒ No

Part 2. Information About You (Petitioner)

1. Alien Registration Number (A-Number) (if any) ▶ A-

2. USCIS Online Account Number (if any) ▶

3. U.S. Social Security Number (if any) ▶ [redacted]

Your Full Name

4.a. Family Name (Last Name) [redacted]

4.b. Given Name (First Name) [redacted]

4.c. Middle Name [redacted]

Part 2. Information About You (Petitioner) (continued)

Other Names Used (if any)

Provide all other names you have ever used, including aliases, maiden name, and nicknames.

5.a. Family Name (Last Name)

5.b. Given Name (First Name)

5.c. Middle Name

Other Information

6. City/Town/Village of Birth
Binghamton

7. Country of Birth
USA

8. Date of Birth (mm/dd/yyyy) 04/05/1967

9. Sex [X] Male [ ] Female

Mailing Address

10.a. In Care Of Name

10.b. Street Number and Name [redacted]

10.c. [X] Apt. [ ] Ste. [ ] Flr. 5C

10.d. City or Town [redacted]

10.e. State CA 10.f. ZIP Code 91745

10.g. Province

10.h. Postal Code

10.i. Country
USA

11. Is your current mailing address the same as your physical address? [X] Yes [ ] No

If you answered "No" to Item Number 11., provide information on your physical address in Item Numbers 12.a. - 13.b.

Address History

Provide your physical addresses for the last five years, whether inside or outside the United States. Provide your current address first if it is different from your mailing address in Item Numbers 10.a. - 10.i.

Physical Address 1

12.a. Street Number and Name

12.b. [ ] Apt. [ ] Ste. [ ] Flr.

12.c. City or Town

12.d. State 12.e. ZIP Code

12.f. Province

12.g. Postal Code

12.h. Country

13.a. Date From (mm/dd/yyyy)

13.b. Date To (mm/dd/yyyy) PRESENT

Physical Address 2

14.a. Street Number and Name [redacted]

14.b. [ ] Apt. [ ] Ste. [ ] Flr.

14.c. City or Town Long Beach

14.d. State CA 14.e. ZIP Code 90810

14.f. Province

14.g. Postal Code

14.h. Country
USA

15.a. Date From (mm/dd/yyyy) 08/01/2016

15.b. Date To (mm/dd/yyyy) 02/10/2018

Your Marital Information

16. How many times have you been married? ▶ 1

17. Current Marital Status

[ ] Single, Never Married [X] Married [ ] Divorced
[ ] Widowed [ ] Separated [ ] Annulled

Part 2. Information About You (Petitioner) (continued)

18. Date of Current Marriage (if currently married) (mm/dd/yyyy) 12/12/2009

Place of Your Current Marriage (if married)

19.a. City or Town Las Vegas

19.b. State NV

19.c. Province

19.d. Country USA

Names of All Your Spouses (if any)

Provide information on your current spouse (if currently married) first and then list all your prior spouses (if any).

Spouse 1

20.a. Family Name (Last Name) [redacted]

20.b. Given Name (First Name) [redacted]

20.c. Middle Name [redacted]

21. Date Marriage Ended (mm/dd/yyyy)

Spouse 2

22.a. Family Name (Last Name)

22.b. Given Name (First Name)

22.c. Middle Name

23. Date Marriage Ended (mm/dd/yyyy)

Information About Your Parents

Parent 1's Information

Full Name of Parent 1

24.a. Family Name (Last Name) [redacted]

24.b. Given Name (First Name) [redacted]

24.c. Middle Name [redacted]

25. Date of Birth (mm/dd/yyyy) 12/21/1927

26. Sex [X] Male [ ] Female

27. Country of Birth USA

28. City/Town/Village of Residence Deceased

29. Country of Residence Deceased

Parent 2's Information

Full Name of Parent 2

30.a. Family Name (Last Name) [redacted]

30.b. Given Name (First Name) [redacted]

30.c. Middle Name [redacted]

31. Date of Birth (mm/dd/yyyy) 07/10/1932

32. Sex [ ] Male [X] Female

33. Country of Birth [redacted]

34. City/Town/Village of Residence [redacted]

35. Country of Residence [redacted]

Additional Information About You (Petitioner)

36. I am a (Select only one box):

[X] U.S. Citizen [ ] Lawful Permanent Resident

If you are a U.S. citizen, complete Item Number 37.

37. My citizenship was acquired through (Select only one box):

[X] Birth in the United States

[ ] Naturalization

[ ] Parents

38. Have you obtained a Certificate of Naturalization or a Certificate of Citizenship? [ ] Yes [X] No

If you answered "Yes" to Item Number 38, complete the following:

39.a. Certificate Number

39.b. Place of Issuance

39.c. Date of Issuance (mm/dd/yyyy)

Part 2. Information About You (Petitioner) (continued)

If you are a lawful permanent resident, complete Item Numbers 40.a. - 41.

40.a. Class of Admission

40.b. Date of Admission (mm/dd/yyyy)

Place of Admission

40.c. City or Town

40.d. State

41. Did you gain lawful permanent resident status through marriage to a U.S. citizen or lawful permanent resident?
☐ Yes ☐ No

Employment History

Provide your employment history for the last five years, whether inside or outside the United States. Provide your current employment first. If you are currently unemployed, type or print "Unemployed" in Item Number 42.

Employer 1

42. Name of Employer/Company: Unemployed

43.a. Street Number and Name

43.b. ☐ Apt. ☐ Ste. ☐ Flr.

43.c. City or Town

43.d. State 43.e. ZIP Code

43.f. Province

43.g. Postal Code

43.h. Country

44. Your Occupation

45.a. Date From (mm/dd/yyyy): 02/2009

45.b. Date To (mm/dd/yyyy): PRESENT

Employer 2

46. Name of Employer/Company

47.a. Street Number and Name

47.b. ☐ Apt. ☐ Ste. ☐ Flr.

47.c. City or Town

47.d. State 47.e. ZIP Code

47.f. Province

47.g. Postal Code

47.h. Country

48. Your Occupation

49.a. Date From (mm/dd/yyyy)

49.b. Date To (mm/dd/yyyy)

Part 3. Biographic Information

NOTE: Provide the biographic information about you, the petitioner.

1. Ethnicity (Select only one box)
   - ☐ Hispanic or Latino
   - ☒ Not Hispanic or Latino

2. Race (Select all applicable boxes)
   - ☒ White
   - ☐ Asian
   - ☐ Black or African American
   - ☐ American Indian or Alaska Native
   - ☐ Native Hawaiian or Other Pacific Islander

3. Height Feet 5 Inches 11

4. Weight Pounds 2 8 0

5. Eye Color (Select only one box)
   - ☐ Black ☐ Blue ☐ Brown
   - ☐ Gray ☒ Green ☐ Hazel
   - ☐ Maroon ☐ Pink ☐ Unknown/Other

Part 3. Biographic Information (continued)

6. Hair Color (Select only one box)

[ ] Bald (No hair) [ ] Black [ ] Blond
[ ] Brown [X] Gray [ ] Red
[ ] Sandy [ ] White [ ] Unknown/Other

Part 4. Information About Beneficiary

1. Alien Registration Number (A-Number) (if any)
► A-

2. USCIS Online Account Number (if any)
►

3. U.S. Social Security Number (if any)
►

Beneficiary's Full Name

4.a. Family Name (Last Name) [redacted]
4.b. Given Name (First Name) [redacted]
4.c. Middle Name [redacted]

Other Names Used (if any)

Provide all other names the beneficiary has ever used, including aliases, maiden name, and nicknames.

5.a. Family Name (Last Name)
5.b. Given Name (First Name)
5.c. Middle Name

Other Information About Beneficiary

6. City/Town/Village of Birth
Cabiao

7. Country of Birth

8. Date of Birth (mm/dd/yyyy) 01/04/1980

9. Sex [ ] Male [X] Female

10. Has anyone else ever filed a petition for the beneficiary?
[ ] Yes [X] No [ ] Unknown

NOTE: Select "Unknown" only if you do not know, and the beneficiary also does not know, if anyone else has ever filed a petition for the beneficiary.

Beneficiary's Physical Address

If the beneficiary lives outside the United States in a home without a street number or name, leave Item Numbers 11.a. and 11.b. blank.

11.a. Street Number and Name [redacted]
11.b. [X] Apt. [ ] Ste. [ ] Flr. 5C
11.c. City or Town [redacted]
11.d. State CA 11.e. ZIP Code 91745
11.f. Province
11.g. Postal Code
11.h. Country
USA

Other Address and Contact Information

Provide the address in the United States where the beneficiary intends to live, if different from Item Numbers 11.a. - 11.h. If the address is the same, type or print "SAME" in Item Number 12.a.

12.a. Street Number and Name SAME
12.b. [ ] Apt. [ ] Ste. [ ] Flr.
12.c. City or Town
12.d. State 12.e. ZIP Code

Provide the beneficiary's address outside the United States, if different from Item Numbers 11.a. - 11.h. If the address is the same, type or print "SAME" in Item Number 13.a.

13.a. Street Number and Name San Fernando Sur
13.b. [ ] Apt. [ ] Ste. [ ] Flr.
13.c. City or Town Cabiao
13.d. Province Nueva Ecija
13.e. Postal Code 3017
13.f. Country
Philippines

14. Daytime Telephone Number (if any)

Part 4. Information About Beneficiary (continued)

15. Mobile Telephone Number (if any) [redacted]

16. Email Address (if any) [redacted]

Beneficiary's Marital Information

17. How many times has the beneficiary been married? 1

18. Current Marital Status

☐ Single, Never Married ☒ Married ☐ Divorced ☐ Widowed ☐ Separated ☐ Annulled

19. Date of Current Marriage (if currently married) (mm/dd/yyyy) 12/12/2009

Place of Beneficiary's Current Marriage (if married)

20.a. City or Town Las Vegas

20.b. State NV

20.c. Province

20.d. Country USA

Names of Beneficiary's Spouses (if any)

Provide information on the beneficiary's current spouse (if currently married) first and then list all the beneficiary's prior spouses (if any).

Spouse 1

21.a. Family Name (Last Name)

21.b. Given Name (First Name)

21.c. Middle Name

22. Date Marriage Ended (mm/dd/yyyy)

Spouse 2

23.a. Family Name (Last Name)

23.b. Given Name (First Name)

23.c. Middle Name

24. Date Marriage Ended (mm/dd/yyyy)

Information About Beneficiary's Family

Provide information about the beneficiary's spouse and children.

Person 1

25.a. Family Name (Last Name) [redacted]

25.b. Given Name (First Name) [redacted]

25.c. Middle Name [redacted]

26. Relationship Spouse

27. Date of Birth (mm/dd/yyyy) 04/05/1967

28. Country of Birth USA

Person 2

29.a. Family Name (Last Name)

29.b. Given Name (First Name)

29.c. Middle Name

30. Relationship

31. Date of Birth (mm/dd/yyyy)

32. Country of Birth

Person 3

33.a. Family Name (Last Name)

33.b. Given Name (First Name)

33.c. Middle Name

34. Relationship

35. Date of Birth (mm/dd/yyyy)

36. Country of Birth

Part 4. Information About Beneficiary (continued)

Person 4

37.a. Family Name (Last Name)

37.b. Given Name (First Name)

37.c. Middle Name

38. Relationship

39. Date of Birth (mm/dd/yyyy)

40. Country of Birth

Person 5

41.a. Family Name (Last Name)

41.b. Given Name (First Name)

41.c. Middle Name

42. Relationship

43. Date of Birth (mm/dd/yyyy)

44. Country of Birth

Beneficiary's Entry Information

45. Was the beneficiary EVER in the United States? ☒ Yes ☐ No

If the beneficiary is currently in the United States, complete Items Numbers 46.a. - 46.d.

46.a. He or she arrived as a (Class of Admission): B-2

46.b. Form I-94 Arrival-Departure Record Number ▶ 5 8 9 6 9 0 5 2 1 1 1

46.c. Date of Arrival (mm/dd/yyyy) 03/30/2005

46.d. Date authorized stay expired, or will expire, as shown on Form I-94 or Form I-95 (mm/dd/yyyy) or type or print "D/S" for Duration of Status 09/ 29/ 2005

47. Passport Number P1774941A

48. Travel Document Number

49. Country of Issuance for Passport or Travel Document

50. Expiration Date for Passport or Travel Document (mm/dd/yyyy) 01/25/2022

Beneficiary's Employment Information

Provide the beneficiary's current employment information (if applicable), even if they are employed outside of the United States. If the beneficiary is currently unemployed, type or print "Unemployed" in Item Number 51.a.

51.a. Name of Current Employer (if applicable) Unemployed

51.b. Street Number and Name

51.c. ☐ Apt. ☐ Ste. ☐ Flr.

51.d. City or Town

51.e. State 51.f. ZIP Code

51.g. Province

51.h. Postal Code

51.i. Country

52. Date Employment Began (mm/dd/yyyy) 03/ 2005

Additional Information About Beneficiary

53. Was the beneficiary EVER in immigration proceedings? ☐ Yes ☒ No

54. If you answered "Yes," select the type of proceedings and provide the location and date of the proceedings.

☐ Removal ☐ Exclusion/Deportation

☐ Rescission ☐ Other Judicial Proceedings

55.a. City or Town

55.b. State

56. Date (mm/dd/yyyy)

Part 4. Information About Beneficiary (continued)

If the beneficiary's native written language does not use Roman letters, type or print his or her name and foreign address in their native written language.

57.a. Family Name (Last Name)

57.b. Given Name (First Name)

57.c. Middle Name

58.a. Street Number and Name

58.b. ☐ Apt. ☐ Ste. ☐ Flr.

58.c. City or Town

58.d. Province

58.e. Postal Code

58.f. Country

If filing for your spouse, provide the last address at which you physically lived together. If you never lived together, type or print, "Never lived together" in Item Number 59.a.

59.a. Street Number and Name

59.b. ☒ Apt. ☐ Ste. ☐ Flr. 5C

59.c. City or Town

59.d. State CA 59.e. ZIP Code 91745

59.f. Province

59.g. Postal Code

59.h. Country USA

60.a. Date From (mm/dd/yyyy) 02/10/2018

60.b. Date To (mm/dd/yyyy) Present

The beneficiary is in the United States and will apply for adjustment of status to that of a lawful permanent resident at the U.S. Citizenship and Immigration Services (USCIS) office in:

61.a. City or Town Los Angeles

61.b. State CA

The beneficiary will not apply for adjustment of status in the United States, but he or she will apply for an immigrant visa abroad at the U.S. Embassy or U.S. Consulate in:

62.a. City or Town

62.b. Province

62.c. Country

NOTE: Choosing a U.S. Embassy or U.S. Consulate outside the country of the beneficiary's last residence does not guarantee that it will accept the beneficiary's case for processing. In these situations, the designated U.S. Embassy or U.S. Consulate has discretion over whether or not to accept the beneficiary's case.

Part 5. Other Information

1. Have you EVER previously filed a petition for this beneficiary or any other alien? ☐ Yes ☒ No

If you answered "Yes," provide the name, place, date of filing, and the result.

2.a. Family Name (Last Name)

2.b. Given Name (First Name)

2.c. Middle Name

3.a. City or Town

3.b. State

4. Date Filed (mm/dd/yyyy)

5. Result (for example, approved, denied, withdrawn)

If you are also submitting separate petitions for other relatives, provide the names of and your relationship to each relative.

Relative 1

6.a. Family Name (Last Name)

6.b. Given Name (First Name)

6.c. Middle Name

7. Relationship

Part 5. Other Information (continued)

Relative 2

8.a. Family Name (Last Name)

8.b. Given Name (First Name)

8.c. Middle Name

9. Relationship

WARNING: USCIS investigates the claimed relationships and verifies the validity of documents you submit. If you falsify a family relationship to obtain a visa, USCIS may seek to have you criminally prosecuted.

PENALTIES: By law, you may be imprisoned for up to 5 years or fined $250,000, or both, for entering into a marriage contract in order to evade any U.S. immigration law. In addition, you may be fined up to $10,000 and imprisoned for up to 5 years, or both, for knowingly and willfully falsifying or concealing a material fact or using any false document in submitting this petition.

Part 6. Petitioner's Statement, Contact Information, Declaration, and Signature

NOTE: Read the Penalties section of the Form I-130 Instructions before completing this part.

Petitioner's Statement

NOTE: Select the box for either Item Number 1.a. or 1.b. If applicable, select the box for Item Number 2.

1.a. [X] I can read and understand English, and I have read and understand every question and instruction on this petition and my answer to every question.

1.b. [ ] The interpreter named in Part 7. read to me every question and instruction on this petition and my answer to every question in

a language in which I am fluent. I understood all of this information as interpreted.

2. [X] At my request, the preparer named in Part 8.,

Christopher A. Reed

prepared this petition for me based only upon information I provided or authorized.

Petitioner's Contact Information

3. Petitioner's Daytime Telephone Number

[redacted]

4. Petitioner's Mobile Telephone Number (if any)

[redacted]

5. Petitioner's Email Address (if any)

[redacted]

Petitioner's Declaration and Certification

Copies of any documents I have submitted are exact photocopies of unaltered, original documents, and I understand that USCIS may require that I submit original documents to USCIS at a later date. Furthermore, I authorize the release of any information from any of my records that USCIS may need to determine my eligibility for the immigration benefit I seek.

I further authorize release of information contained in this petition, in supporting documents, and in my USCIS records to other entities and persons where necessary for the administration and enforcement of U.S. immigration laws.

I understand that USCIS may require me to appear for an appointment to take my biometrics (fingerprints, photograph, and/or signature) and, at that time, if I am required to provide biometrics, I will be required to sign an oath reaffirming that:

1) I provided or authorized all of the information contained in, and submitted with, my petition;

2) I reviewed and understood all of the information in, and submitted with, my petition; and

3) All of this information was complete, true, and correct at the time of filing.

I certify, under penalty of perjury, that all of the information in my petition and any document submitted with it were provided or authorized by me, that I reviewed and understand all of the information contained in, and submitted with, my petition, and that all of this information is complete, true, and correct.

Petitioner's Signature

6.a. Petitioner's Signature (sign in ink)

[signature]

6.b. Date of Signature (mm/dd/yyyy) 7/19/18

NOTE TO ALL PETITIONERS: If you do not completely fill out this petition or fail to submit required documents listed in the Instructions, USCIS may deny your petition.

Part 7. Interpreter's Contact Information, Certification, and Signature

Provide the following information about the interpreter if you used one.

Interpreter's Full Name

1.a. Interpreter's Family Name (Last Name)

1.b. Interpreter's Given Name (First Name)

2. Interpreter's Business or Organization Name (if any)

Interpreter's Mailing Address

3.a. Street Number and Name

3.b. ☐ Apt. ☐ Ste. ☐ Flr.

3.c. City or Town

3.d. State 3.e. ZIP Code

3.f. Province

3.g. Postal Code

3.h. Country

Interpreter's Contact Information

4. Interpreter's Daytime Telephone Number

5. Interpreter's Mobile Telephone Number (if any)

6. Interpreter's Email Address (if any)

Interpreter's Certification

I certify, under penalty of perjury, that:

I am fluent in English and

which is the same language provided in Part 6., Item Number 1.b., and I have read to this petitioner in the identified language every question and instruction on this petition and his or her answer to every question. The petitioner informed me that he or she understands every instruction, question, and answer on the petition, including the Petitioner's Declaration and Certification, and has verified the accuracy of every answer.

Interpreter's Signature

7.a. Interpreter's Signature (sign in ink)

7.b. Date of Signature (mm/dd/yyyy)

Part 8. Contact Information, Declaration, and Signature of the Person Preparing this Petition, if Other Than the Petitioner

Provide the following information about the preparer.

Preparer's Full Name

1.a. Preparer's Family Name (Last Name)
Reed

1.b. Preparer's Given Name (First Name)
Christopher

2. Preparer's Business or Organization Name (if any)
Law Offices of Brian D. Lerner, APC

Preparer's Mailing Address

3.a. Street Number and Name 3233 E. Broadway

3.b. ☐ Apt. ☐ Ste. ☐ Flr.

3.c. City or Town Long Beach

3.d. State CA 3.e. ZIP Code 90803

3.f. Province

3.g. Postal Code

3.h. Country
USA

Part 8. Contact Information, Declaration, and Signature of the Person Preparing this Petition, if Other Than the Petitioner (continued)

Preparer's Contact Information

4. Preparer's Daytime Telephone Number

5624950554

5. Preparer's Mobile Telephone Number (if any)

6. Preparer's Email Address (if any)

creed@elmmigration.org

Preparer's Statement

7.a. [ ] I am not an attorney or accredited representative but have prepared this petition on behalf of the petitioner and with the petitioner's consent.

7.b. [X] I am an attorney or accredited representative and my representation of the petitioner in this case [X] extends [ ] does not extend beyond the preparation of this petition.

NOTE: If you are an attorney or accredited representative whose representation extends beyond preparation of this petition, you may be obliged to submit a completed Form G-28, Notice of Entry of Appearance as Attorney or Accredited Representative, with this petition.

Preparer's Certification

By my signature, I certify, under penalty of perjury, that I prepared this petition at the request of the petitioner. The petitioner then reviewed this completed petition and informed me that he or she understands all of the information contained in, and submitted with, his or her petition, including the Petitioner's Declaration and Certification, and that all of this information is complete, true, and correct. I completed this petition based only on information that the petitioner provided to me or authorized me to obtain or use.

Preparer's Signature

8.a. Preparer's Signature (sign in ink)

8.b. Date of Signature (mm/dd/yyyy) 7/23/18

Part 9. Additional Information

If you need extra space to provide any additional information within this petition, use the space below. If you need more space than what is provided, you may make copies of this page to complete and file with this petition or attach a separate sheet of paper. Type or print your name and A-Number (if any) at the top of each sheet; indicate the **Page Number, Part Number**, and **Item Number** to which your answer refers; and sign and date each sheet.

1.a. Family Name (Last Name) [redacted]

1.b. Given Name (First Name) [redacted]

1.c. Middle Name [redacted]

2. A-Number (if any) ▶ A-

3.a. Page Number 2 3.b. Part Number 2 3.c. Item Number 14a-15b

3.d.

ADDITIONAL PRIOR ADDRESSES OF PETITIONER

DATES: 06/2014-08/2016
1521 Rose Court
West Covina, CA 91791

DATES: 02/2013-06/2014
2648 Erica Avenue
West Covina, CA 91792

4.a. Page Number 4.b. Part Number 4.c. Item Number

4.d.

5.a. Page Number 5.b. Part Number 5.c. Item Number

5.d.

6.a. Page Number 6.b. Part Number 6.c. Item Number

6.d.

7.a. Page Number 7.b. Part Number 7.c. Item Number

7.d.

Supplemental Information for Spouse Beneficiary

Department of Homeland Security
U.S. Citizenship and Immigration Services

USCIS
Form I-130A
OMB No. 1615-0012
Expires 07/31/2018

To be completed by an attorney or accredited representative (if any).			
☒ Select this box if Form G-28 is attached.	Volag Number (if any)	Attorney State Bar Number (if applicable): 235438	Attorney or Accredited Representative USCIS Online Account Number (if any)

▶ START HERE - Type or print in black ink.

The purpose of this form is to collect additional information for a spouse beneficiary of Form I-130, Petition for Alien Relative. If your spouse is a U.S. citizen, lawful permanent resident, or non-citizen U.S. national who is filing Form I-130 on your behalf, you must complete and sign Form I-130A, Supplemental Information for Spouse Beneficiary, and submit it with the Form I-130 filed by your spouse. If you reside overseas, you still must complete Form I-130A, but you do not need to sign the form.

Part 1. Information About You (Spouse Beneficiary)

1. Alien Registration Number (A-Number) (if any) ▶ A-

2. USCIS Online Account Number (if any) ▶

Your Full Name

3.a. Family Name (Last Name) [redacted]
3.b. Given Name (First Name) [redacted]
3.c. Middle Name [redacted]

Address History

Provide your physical addresses for the last five years, whether inside or outside the United States. Provide your current address first. If you need extra space to complete this section, use the space provided in Part 7. Additional Information.

Physical Address 1

4.a. Street Number and Name [redacted]
4.b. ☒ Apt. ☐ Ste. ☐ Flr. 5C
4.c. City or Town [redacted]
4.d. State CA 4.e. ZIP Code 91745
4.f. Province
4.g. Postal Code
4.h. Country

5.a. Date From (mm/dd/yyyy) 02/10/2018
5.b. Date To (mm/dd/yyyy) PRESENT

Physical Address 2

6.a. Street Number and Name [redacted]
6.b. ☐ Apt. ☐ Ste. ☐ Flr.
6.c. City or Town Long Beach
6.d. State CA 6.e. ZIP Code 90810
6.f. Province
6.g. Postal Code
6.h. Country USA

7.a. Date From (mm/dd/yyyy) 08/01/2016
7.b. Date To (mm/dd/yyyy) 02/10/2018

Last Physical Address Outside the United States

Provide your last address outside the United States of more than one year (even if listed above).

8.a. Street Number and Name San Fernando Sur
8.b. ☐ Apt. ☐ Ste. ☐ Flr.
8.c. City or Town Cabiao
8.d. Province
8.e. Postal Code 3107

Part 1. Information About You (The Spouse Beneficiary)

9.a. Date From (mm/dd/yyyy) 01/04/1980

9.b. Date To (mm/dd/yyyy) 03/30/2005

Information About Parent 1

Full Name of Parent 1

10.a. Family Name (Maiden Name) [redacted]

10.b. Given Name (First Name) [redacted]

10.c. Middle Name

11. Date of Birth (mm/dd/yyyy) 10/21/1947

12. Sex ☐ Male ☒ Female

13. City/Town/Village of Birth

14. Country of Birth

15. City/Town/Village of Residence

Rowland Heights

16. Country of Residence

USA

Information About Parent 2

Full Name of Parent 2

17.a. Family Name (Last Name) [redacted]

17.b. Given Name (First Name) [redacted]

17.c. Middle Name [redacted]

18. Date of Birth (mm/dd/yyyy) 10/18/1943

19. Sex ☒ Male ☐ Female

20. City/Town/Village of Birth

21. Country of Birth

22. City/Town/Village of Residence

Rowland Heights

Part 2. Information About Your Employment

Provide your employment history for the last five years, whether inside or outside the United States. Provide your current employment first. If you are currently unemployed, type or print "Unemployed" in **Item Number 1.** below. If you need extra space to complete this section, use the space provided in **Part 7. Additional Information.**

Employment History

Employer 1

1. Name of Employer/Company

Unemployed

2.a. Street Number and Name

2.b. ☐ Apt. ☐ Ste. ☐ Flr.

2.c. City or Town

2.d. State 2.e. ZIP Code

2.f. Province

2.g. Postal Code

2.h. Country

3. Your Occupation

4.a. Date From (mm/dd/yyyy) 08/2005

4.b. Date To (mm/dd/yyyy) PRESENT

Employer 2

5. Name of Employer/Company

6.a. Street Number and Name

6.b. ☐ Apt. ☐ Ste. ☐ Flr.

6.c. City or Town

6.d. State 6.e. ZIP Code

6.f. Province

6.g. Postal Code

6.h. Country

Part 2. Information About Your Employment (continued)

7. Your Occupation

8.a. Date From (mm/dd/yyyy)

8.b. Date To (mm/dd/yyyy)

Part 3. Information About Your Employment Outside the United States

Provide your last occupation outside the United States if not shown above. If you never worked outside the United States, provide this information in the space provided in **Part 7. Additional Information**.

1. Name of Employer/Company
NONE

2.a. Street Number and Name

2.b. ☐ Apt. ☐ Ste. ☐ Flr.

2.c. City or Town

2.d. State 2.e. ZIP Code

2.f. Province

2.g. Postal Code

2.h. Country

3. Your Occupation

4.a. Date From (mm/dd/yyyy)

4.b. Date To (mm/dd/yyyy)

Part 4. Spouse Beneficiary's Statement, Contact Information, Certification, and Signature

NOTE: Read the **Penalties** section of the Form I-130 and Form I-130A Instructions before completing this part.

Spouse Beneficiary's Statement

NOTE: Select the box for either **Item Number 1.a.** or **1.b.** If applicable, select the box for **Item Number 2.**

1.a. ☒ I can read and understand English, and I have read

1.b. ☐ The interpreter named in Part 5. read to me every question and instruction on this form and my answer to every question in

a language in which I am fluent, and I understood everything.

2. ☒ At my request, the preparer name in Part 6.,
Christopher A. Reed,
prepared this form for me based only upon information I provided or authorized.

Spouse Beneficiary's Contact Information

3. Spouse Beneficiary's Daytime Telephone Number
(323) 404-2220

4. Spouse Beneficiary's Mobile Telephone Number (if any)
[redacted]

5. Spouse Beneficiary's Email Address (if any)

Spouse Beneficiary's Certification

Copies of any documents I have submitted are exact photocopies of unaltered, original documents, and I understand that USCIS may require that I submit original documents to USCIS at a later date. Furthermore, I authorize the release of any information from any of my records that USCIS may need to determine my eligibility for the immigration benefit I seek.

I further authorize release of information contained in this form, in supporting documents, and in my USCIS records to other entities and persons where necessary for the administration and enforcement of U.S. immigration laws.

I certify, under penalty of perjury, that I provided or authorized all of the information in this form, I understand all of the information contained in, and submitted with, my form, and that all of this information is complete, true, and correct.

Spouse Beneficiary's Signature

6.a. Spouse Beneficiary's Signature
➡ [redacted]

6.b. Date of Signature (mm/dd/yyyy) 7/19/18

NOTE TO ALL SPOUSE BENEFICIARIES: If you do not completely fill out this form or fail to submit required documents listed in the Instructions, USCIS may deny the Form I-130 filed on your behalf.

Part 5. Interpreter's Contact Information, Certification, and Signature

Provide the following information about the interpreter you used to complete Form I-130A if he or she is different from the interpreter used to complete the Form I-130 filed on your behalf.

Interpreter's Full Name

1.a. Interpreter's Family Name (Last Name)

1.b. Interpreter's Given Name (First Name)

2. Interpreter's Business or Organization Name (if any)

Interpreter's Mailing Address

3.a. Street Number and Name

3.b. ☐ Apt. ☐ Ste. ☐ Flr.

3.c. City or Town

3.d. State 3.e. ZIP Code

3.f. Province

3.g. Postal Code

3.h. Country

Interpreter's Contact Information

4. Interpreter's Daytime Telephone Number

5. Interpreter's Mobile Telephone Number (if any)

6. Interpreter's Email Address (if any)

Interpreter's Certification

I certify, under penalty of perjury, that:

I am fluent in English and ______,

which is the same language provided in **Part 4., Item Number 1.b.**, and I have read to this spouse beneficiary in the identified language every question and instruction on this form and his or her answer to every question. The spouse beneficiary informed me that he or she understands every instruction, question, and answer on the form, including the **Spouse Beneficiary's Certification**, and has verified the accuracy of every answer.

Interpreter's Signature

7.a. Interpreter's Signature

7.b. Date of Signature (mm/dd/yyyy)

Part 6. Contact Information, Declaration, and Signature of the Person Preparing this Form, if Other Than the Spouse Beneficiary

Provide the following information about the preparer you used to complete Form I-130A if he or she is different from the preparer used to complete the Form I-130 filed on your behalf.

Preparer's Full Name

1.a. Preparer's Family Name (Last Name)
Reed

1.b. Preparer's Given Name (First Name)
Christopher

2. Preparer's Business or Organization Name (if any)
Law Offices of Brian D. Lerner, APC

Preparer's Mailing Address

3.a. Street Number and Name
3233 E. Broadway

3.b. ☐ Apt. ☐ Ste. ☐ Flr.

3.c. City or Town
Long Beach

3.d. State CA 3.e. ZIP Code 90803

3.f. Province

3.g. Postal Code

3.h. Country

Part 6. Contact Information, Declaration, and Signature of the Person Preparing this Form, if Other Than the Spouse Beneficiary (continued)

Preparer's Contact Information

4. Preparer's Daytime Telephone Number

(562) 495-0554

5. Preparer's Mobile Telephone Number (if any)

6. Preparer's Email Address (if any)

creed@californiaimmigration.us

Preparer's Statement

7.a. ☐ I am not an attorney or accredited representative but have prepared this form on behalf of the spouse beneficiary and with the spouse beneficiary's consent

7.b. ☒ I am an attorney or accredited representative and my representation of the spouse beneficiary in this case ☒ extends ☐ does not extend beyond the preparation of this form.

NOTE: If you are an attorney or accredited representative whose representation extends beyond preparation of this form, you may be obliged to submit a completed Form G-28, Notice of Entry of Appearance as Attorney or Accredited Representative, with this form.

Preparer's Certification

By my signature, I certify, under penalty of perjury, that I prepared this form at the request of the spouse beneficiary. The spouse beneficiary then reviewed this completed form and informed me that he or she understands all of the information contained in, and submitted with, his or her form, including the **Spouse Beneficiary's Certification**, and that all of this information is complete, true, and correct. I completed this form based only on information that the spouse beneficiary provided to me or authorized me to obtain or use.

Preparer's Signature

8.a. Preparer's Signature

8.b. Date of Signature (mm/dd/yyyy) 7/03/18

Part 7. Additional Information

If you need extra space to provide any additional information within this form, use the space below. If you need more space than what is provided, you may make copies of this page to complete and file with this form or attach a separate sheet of paper. Type or print your name and A-Number (if any) at the top of each sheet; indicate the **Page Number**, **Part Number**, and **Item Number** to which your answer refers; and sign and date each sheet.

1.a. Family Name (Last Name) [redacted]

1.b. Given Name (First Name) [redacted]

1.c. Middle Name [redacted]

2. A-Number (if any) ► A-

3.a. Page Number 3.b. Part Number 3.c. Item Number

3.d.

4.a. Page Number 4.b. Part Number 4.c. Item Number

4.d.

5.a. Page Number 5.b. Part Number 5.c. Item Number

5.d.

6.a. Page Number 6.b. Part Number 6.c. Item Number

6.d.

7.a. Page Number 7.b. Part Number 7.c. Item Number

7.d.

Addendum

[redacted] Form: I-130A (Page 1)

Part 1: Additional Address History:

Address: 1521 Rose Court, City: West Covina, State: CA, Zip Code: 91791, County: Los Angeles, Country: USA, Date From: 6/15/2014 Date To: 8/1/2016;

Address: 2648 Erica Avenue, City: West Covina, State: CA, Zip Code: 91792, County: , Country: USA, Date From: 2/1/2013 Date To: 6/15/2014;

Application to Register Permanent Residence or Adjust Status

Department of Homeland Security
U.S. Citizenship and Immigration Services

USCIS
Form I-485
OMB No. 1615-0023
Expires 06/30/2019

For USCIS Use Only		
Preference Category:	Receipt	Action Block
Country Chargeable:		
Priority Date:		
Date Form I-693 Received:		
☐ Applicant Interviewed ☐ Interview Waived Date of Initial Interview: ______ Lawful Permanent Resident as of: ______	Section of Law ☐ INA 209(a) ☐ INA 249 ☐ INA 209(b) ☐ Sec. 13, Act of 9/11/57 ☐ INA 245(a) ☐ Cuban Adjustment Act ☐ INA 245(i) ☐ Other ______ ☐ INA 245(m)	

To be completed by an attorney or accredited representative (if any).			
☒ Select this box if Form G-28 is attached.	Volag Number (if any)	Attorney State Bar Number (if applicable) 235438	Attorney or Accredited Representative USCIS Online Account Number (if any)

► START HERE - Type or print in black ink. A-Number ► A-

NOTE TO ALL APPLICANTS: If you do not completely fill out this application or fail to submit required documents listed in the Instructions, U.S. Citizenship and Immigration Services (USCIS) may deny your application.

Part 1. Information About You (Person applying for lawful permanent residence)

Your Current Legal Name (do not provide a nickname)

1.a. Family Name (Last Name) [redacted]
1.b. Given Name (First Name) [redacted]
1.c. Middle Name [redacted]

Other Names You Have Used Since Birth (if applicable)

NOTE: Provide all other names you have ever used, including your family name at birth, other legal names, nicknames, aliases, and assumed names. If you need extra space to complete this section, use the space provided in Part 14. **Additional Information**.

2.a. Family Name (Last Name)
2.b. Given Name (First Name)
2.c. Middle Name

3.a. Family Name (Last Name)
3.b. Given Name (First Name)
3.c. Middle Name

4.a. Family Name (Last Name)
4.b. Given Name (First Name)
4.c. Middle Name

Other Information About You

5. Date of Birth (mm/dd/yyyy) 01/04/1980

NOTE: In addition to providing your actual date of birth, include any other dates of birth you have used in connection with any legal names or non-legal names in the space provided in Part 14. **Additional Information**.

6. Sex ☐ Male ☒ Female

7. City or Town of Birth
Cabiao

A-Number ▶ A-

Part 1. Information About You (Person applying for lawful permanent residence) (continued)

8. Country of Birth

9. Country of Citizenship or Nationality

10. Alien Registration Number (A-Number) (if any)
▶ A-

NOTE: If you have **EVER** used other A-Numbers, include the additional A-Numbers in the space provided in **Part 14. Additional Information**

11. USCIS Online Account Number (if any)
▶

12. U.S. Social Security Number (if any)
▶

U.S. Mailing Address

13.a. In Care Of Name (if any)

13.b. Street Number and Name [redacted]

13.c. ☒ Apt ☐ Ste ☐ Flr 5C

13.d. City or Town [redacted]

13.e. State CA 13.f. ZIP Code 91745

Alternate and/or Safe Mailing Address

If you are applying based on the Violence Against Women Act (VAWA) or as a special immigrant juvenile, human trafficking victim (T nonimmigrant), or victim of a qualifying crime (U nonimmigrant) and you do not want USCIS to send notices about this application to your home, you may provide an alternative and/or safe mailing address.

14.a. In Care Of Name (if any)

14.b. Street Number and Name

14.c. ☐ Apt ☐ Ste ☐ Flr

14.d. City or Town

14.e. State 14.f. ZIP Code

Recent Immigration History

Provide the information for **Item Numbers 15. - 19.** if you last entered the United States using a passport or travel document.

15. Passport Number Used at Last Arrival

16. Travel Document Number Used at Last Arrival

17. Expiration Date of this Passport or Travel Document (mm/dd/yyyy) 04/18/2006

18. Country that Issued this Passport or Travel Document

19. Nonimmigrant Visa Number from this Passport (if any)
2c012776400c08

Place of Last Arrival into the United States

20.a. City or Town
Los Angeles

20.b. State CA

21. Date of Last Arrival (mm/dd/yyyy) 03/30/2005

When I last arrived in the United States, I:

22.a. ☒ Was inspected at a port of entry and admitted as (for example, exchange visitor, visitor, waived through, temporary worker, student)
Visitor

22.b. ☐ Was inspected at a port of entry and paroled as (for example, humanitarian parole, Cuban parole)

22.c. ☐ Came into the United States without admission or parole

22.d. ☐ Other

If you were issued a Form I-94 Arrival-Departure Record Number:

23.a. Form I-94 Arrival-Departure Record Number
▶ [redacted]

23.b. Expiration Date of Authorized Stay Shown on Form I-94 (mm/dd/yyyy) 09/29/2005

23.c. Status on Form I-94 (for example, class of admission, or paroled, if paroled)
B-2

A-Number ► A-

Part 1. Information About You (Person applying for lawful permanent residence) (continued)

24. What is your current immigration status (if it has changed since your arrival)?

Unlawful Status

Provide your name exactly as it appears on your Form I-94 (if any).

25.a. Family Name (Last Name) [redacted]

25.b. Given Name (First Name) [redacted]

25.c. Middle Name [redacted]

Part 2. Application Type or Filing Category

NOTE: Attach a copy of the Form I-797 receipt or approval notice for the underlying petition or application, as appropriate.

I am applying to register lawful permanent residence or adjust status to that of a lawful permanent resident based on the following immigrant category (select **only one** box). (See the Form I-485 Instructions for more information, including any **Additional Instructions** that relate to the immigrant category you select.):

1.a. **Family-based**

- [x] Immediate relative of a U.S. citizen, Form I-130
- [ ] Other relative of a U.S. citizen or relative of a lawful permanent resident under the family-based preference categories, Form I-130
- [ ] Person admitted to the United States as a fiancé(e) or child of a fiancé(e) of a U.S. citizen, Form I-129F (K-1/K-2 Nonimmigrant)
- [ ] Widow or widower of a U.S. citizen, Form I-360
- [ ] VAWA self-petitioner, Form I-360

1.b. **Employment-based**

- [ ] Alien worker, Form I-140
- [ ] Alien entrepreneur, Form I-526

1.c. **Special Immigrant**

- [ ] Religious worker, Form I-360
- [ ] Special immigrant juvenile, Form I-360
- [ ] Certain Afghan or Iraqi national, Form I-360
- [ ] Certain international broadcaster, Form I-360
- [ ] Certain G-4 international organization or family member or NATO-6 employee or family member, Form I-360

1.d. **Asylee or Refugee**

- [ ] Asylum status (INA section 208), Form I-589 or Form I-730
- [ ] Refugee status (INA section 207), Form I-590 or Form I-730

1.e. **Human Trafficking Victim or Crime Victim**

- [ ] Human trafficking victim (T Nonimmigrant), Form I-914 or derivative family member, Form I-914A
- [ ] Crime victim (U Nonimmigrant), Form I-918, derivative family member, Form I-918A, or qualifying family member, Form I-929

1.f. **Special Programs Based on Certain Public Laws**

- [ ] The Cuban Adjustment Act
- [ ] The Cuban Adjustment Act for battered spouses and children
- [ ] Dependent status under the Haitian Refugee Immigrant Fairness Act
- [ ] Dependent status under the Haitian Refugee Immigrant Fairness Act for battered spouses and children
- [ ] Lautenberg Parolees
- [ ] Diplomats or high ranking officials unable to return home (Section 13 of the Act of September 11, 1957)
- [ ] Indochinese Parole Adjustment Act of 2000

1.g. **Additional Options**

- [ ] Diversity Visa program
- [ ] Continuous residence in the United States since before January 1, 1972 ("Registry")
- [ ] Individual born in the United States under diplomatic status
- [ ] Other eligibility

2. Are you applying for adjustment based on the Immigration and Nationality Act (INA) section 245(i)? [ ] Yes [x] No

NOTE: If you answered "Yes" to **Item Number 2.**, you must have selected a family-based, employment-based, special immigrant, or Diversity Visa immigrant category listed above in **Item Numbers 1.a. - 1.g.** as the basis for your application for adjustment of status. Fill out the rest of this application and Supplement A to Form I-485, Adjustment of Status Under Section 245(i) (Supplement A). For detailed filing instructions, read the Form I-485 Instructions (including any **Additional Instructions** that relate to the immigrant category that you selected in **Item Numbers 1.a. - 1.g.**) and Supplement A Instructions.

A-Number ▶ A-

Part 2. Application Type or Filing Category (continued)

Information About Your Immigrant Category

If you are the principal applicant, provide the following information.

3. Receipt Number of Underlying Petition (if any)

4. Priority Date from Underlying Petition (if any) (mm/dd/yyyy)

If you are a derivative applicant (the spouse or unmarried child under 21 years of age of a principal applicant), provide the following information for the principal applicant.

Principal Applicant's Name

5.a. Family Name (Last Name)

5.b. Given Name (First Name)

5.c. Middle Name

6. Principal Applicant's A-Number (if any) ▶ A-

7. Principal Applicant's Date of Birth (mm/dd/yyyy)

8. Receipt Number of Principal's Underlying Petition (if any) ▶

9. Priority Date of Principal Applicant's Underlying Petition (if any) (mm/dd/yyyy)

Part 3. Additional Information About You

1. Have you ever applied for an immigrant visa to obtain permanent resident status at a U.S. Embassy or U.S. Consulate abroad? ☐ Yes ☒ No

If you answered "Yes" to Item Number 1., complete Item Numbers 2.a. - 4. below. If you need extra space to complete this section, use the space provided in Part 14. Additional Information.

Location of U.S. Embassy or U.S. Consulate

2.a. City

2.b. Country

3. Decision (for example, approved, refused, denied, withdrawn)

4. Date of Decision (mm/dd/yyyy)

Address History

Provide physical addresses for everywhere you have lived during the last five years, whether inside or outside the United States. Provide your current address first. If you need extra space to complete this section, use the space provided in **Part 14. Additional Information.**

Physical Address 1 (current address)

5.a. Street Number and Name [redacted]

5.b. ☒ Apt ☐ Ste. ☐ Flr. 5C

5.c. City or Town [redacted]

5.d. State CA 5.e. ZIP Code 91745

5.f. Province

5.g. Postal Code

5.h. Country USA

Dates of Residence

6.a. From (mm/dd/yyyy) 02/10/2018

6.b. To (mm/dd/yyyy) Present

Physical Address 2

7.a. Street Number and Name [redacted]

7.b. ☐ Apt ☐ Ste. ☐ Flr.

7.c. City or Town Long Beach

7.d. State CA 7.e. ZIP Code 90810

7.f. Province

7.g. Postal Code

7.h. Country USA

A-Number ► A-

Part 3. Additional Information About You (continued)

Dates of Residence

8.a. From (mm/dd/yyyy) 08/01/2016

8.b. To (mm/dd/yyyy) 02/10/2018

Provide your most recent address outside the United States where you lived for more than one year (if not already listed above).

9.a. Street Number and Name [redacted]

9.b. ☐ Apt. ☐ Ste. ☐ Flr.

9.c. City or Town [redacted]

9.d. State 9.e. ZIP Code

9.f. Province [redacted]

9.g. Postal Code 3107

9.h. Country [redacted]

Dates of Residence

10.a. From (mm/dd/yyyy) 01/04/1980

10.b. To (mm/dd/yyyy) 03/30/2005

Employment History

Provide your employment history for the last five years, whether inside or outside the United States. Provide the most recent employment first. If you need extra space to complete this section, use the space provided in **Part 14. Additional Information**.

Employer 1 (current or most recent)

11. Name of Employer or Company Unemployed

Address of Employer or Company

12.a. Street Number and Name

12.b. ☐ Apt. ☐ Ste. ☐ Flr.

12.c. City or Town

12.d. State 12.e. ZIP Code

12.f. Province

12.g. Postal Code

12.h. Country

13. Your Occupation

Dates of Employment

14.a. From (mm/dd/yyyy) 03/2005

14.b. To (mm/dd/yyyy) Present

Employer 2

15. Name of Employer or Company

Address of Employer or Company

16.a. Street Number and Name

16.b. ☐ Apt. ☐ Ste. ☐ Flr.

16.c. City or Town

16.d. State 16.e. ZIP Code

16.f. Province

16.g. Postal Code

16.h. Country

17. Your Occupation

Dates of Employment

18.a. From (mm/dd/yyyy)

18.b. To (mm/dd/yyyy)

A-Number ▶ A-

Part 3. Additional Information About You (continued)

Provide your most recent employment outside of the United States (if not already listed above).

19. Name of Employer or Company: NONE

Address of Employer or Company

20.a. Street Number and Name:

20.b. ☐ Apt. ☐ Ste. ☐ Flr.

20.c. City or Town:

20.d. State: 20.e. ZIP Code:

20.f. Province:

20.g. Postal Code:

20.h. Country:

21. Your Occupation:

Dates of Employment

22.a. From (mm/dd/yyyy):

22.b. To (mm/dd/yyyy):

Part 4. Information About Your Parents

Information About Your Parent 1

Parent 1's Legal Name

1.a. Family Name (Last Name): [redacted]

1.b. Given Name (First Name): Clarita [redacted]

1.c. Middle Name: Galang

Parent 1's Name at Birth (if different than above)

2.a. Family Name (Last Name):

2.b. Given Name (First Name):

2.c. Middle Name:

3. Date of Birth (mm/dd/yyyy): 10/21/1947

4. Sex ☐ Male ☒ Female

5. City or Town of Birth: [redacted]

6. Country of Birth:

7. Current City or Town of Residence (if living): Rowland Heights

8. Current Country of Residence (if living): USA

Information About Your Parent 2

Parent 2's Legal Name

9.a. Family Name (Last Name): [redacted]

9.b. Given Name (First Name): [redacted]

9.c. Middle Name: [redacted]

Parent 2's Name at Birth (if different than above)

10.a. Family Name (Last Name):

10.b. Given Name (First Name):

10.c. Middle Name:

11. Date of Birth (mm/dd/yyyy): 10/18/1943

12. Sex ☒ Male ☐ Female

13. City or Town of Birth: [redacted]

14. Country of Birth: [redacted]

15. Current City or Town of Residence (if living): [redacted]

16. Current Country of Residence (if living): USA

A-Number ▶ A-

Part 5. Information About Your Marital History

1. What is your current marital status?

☐ Single, Never Married ☒ Married ☐ Divorced

☐ Widowed ☐ Marriage Annulled

☐ Legally Separated

2. If you are married, is your spouse a current member of the U.S. armed forces or U.S. Coast Guard?

☐ N/A ☐ Yes ☒ No

3. How many times have you been married (including annulled marriages and marriages to the same person)?

1

Information About Your Current Marriage (including if you are legally separated)

If you are currently married, provide the following information about your current spouse.

Current Spouse's Legal Name

4.a. Family Name (Last Name) [redacted]

4.b. Given Name (First Name) [redacted]

4.c. Middle Name [redacted]

5. A-Number (if any) ▶ A-

6. Current Spouse's Date of Birth (mm/dd/yyyy) 04/05/1967

7. Date of Marriage to Current Spouse (mm/dd/yyyy) 12/12/2009

Current Spouse's Place of Birth

8.a. City or Town: Binghamton

8.b. State or Province: New York

8.c. Country: USA

Place of Marriage to Current Spouse

9.a. City or Town: Las Vegas

9.b. State or Province: NV

9.c. Country: USA

10. Is your current spouse applying with you?

☐ Yes ☒ No

Information About Prior Marriages (if any)

If you have been married before, whether in the United States or in any other country, provide the following information about your prior spouse. If you have had more than one previous marriage, use the space provided in Part 14. **Additional Information** to provide the information below.

Prior Spouse's Legal Name (provide family name before marriage)

11.a. Family Name (Last Name)

11.b. Given Name (First Name)

11.c. Middle Name

12. Prior Spouse's Date of Birth (mm/dd/yyyy)

13. Date of Marriage to Prior Spouse (mm/dd/yyyy)

Place of Marriage to Prior Spouse

14.a. City or Town

14.b. State or Province

14.c. Country

15. Date Marriage with Prior Spouse Legally Ended (mm/dd/yyyy)

A-Number ▶ A-

Part 5. Information About Your Marital History (continued)

Place Where Marriage with Prior Spouse Legally Ended

16.a. City or Town

16.b. State or Province

16.c. Country

Part 6. Information About Your Children

1. Indicate the total number of ALL living children (including adult sons and daughters) that you have.

NOTE: The term "children" includes all biological or legally adopted children, as well as current stepchildren, of any age, whether born in the United States or other countries, married or unmarried, living with you or elsewhere and includes any missing children and those born to you outside of marriage. 0

Provide the following information for each of your children. If you have more than three children, use the space provided in **Part 14. Additional Information**.

Child 1

Current Legal Name

2.a. Family Name (Last Name)

2.b. Given Name (First Name)

2.c. Middle Name

3. A-Number (if any) ▶ A-

4. Date of Birth (mm/dd/yyyy)

5. Country of Birth

6. Is this child applying with you? ☐ Yes ☐ No

Child 2

Current Legal Name

7.a. Family Name (Last Name)

7.b. Given Name (First Name)

7.c. Middle Name

8. A-Number (if any) ▶ A-

9. Date of Birth (mm/dd/yyyy)

10. Country of Birth

11. Is this child applying with you? ☐ Yes ☐ No

Child 3

Current Legal Name

12.a. Family Name (Last Name)

12.b. Given Name (First Name)

12.c. Middle Name

13. A-Number (if any) ▶ A-

14. Date of Birth (mm/dd/yyyy)

15. Country of Birth

16. Is this child applying with you? ☐ Yes ☐ No

Part 7. Biographic Information

1. Ethnicity (Select only one box)

☐ Hispanic or Latino

☒ Not Hispanic or Latino

2. Race (Select all applicable boxes)

☐ White

☒ Asian

☐ Black or African American

☐ American Indian or Alaska Native

☐ Native Hawaiian or Other Pacific Islander

A-Number ▶ A-

Part 7. Biographic Information (continued)

3. Height Feet 5 Inches 4

4. Weight Pounds 1 3 5

5. Eye Color (Select only one box)

[X] Black [ ] Blue [ ] Brown
[ ] Gray [ ] Green [ ] Hazel
[ ] Maroon [ ] Pink [ ] Unknown/Other

6. Hair Color (Select only one box)

[ ] Bald (No hair) [X] Black [ ] Blond
[ ] Brown [ ] Gray [ ] Red
[ ] Sandy [ ] White [ ] Unknown/Other

Part 8. General Eligibility and Inadmissibility Grounds

1. Have you EVER been a member of, involved in, or in any way associated with any organization, association, fund, foundation, party, club, society, or similar group in the United States or in any other location in the world including any military service? [ ] Yes [X] No

If you answered "Yes" to **Item Number 1.**, complete **Item Numbers 2. - 13.b.** below. If you need extra space to complete this section, use the space provided in **Part 14. Additional Information**. If you answered "No," but are unsure of your answer, provide an explanation of the events and circumstances in the space provided in **Part 14. Additional Information**.

Organization 1

2. Name of Organization
NONE

3.a. City or Town

3.b. State or Province

3.c. Country

4. Nature of Group

Dates of Membership or Dates of Involvement

5.a. From (mm/dd/yyyy)

5.b. To (mm/dd/yyyy)

Organization 2

6. Name of Organization

7.a. City or Town

7.b. State or Province

7.c. Country

8. Nature of Group

Dates of Membership or Dates of Involvement

9.a. From (mm/dd/yyyy)

9.b. To (mm/dd/yyyy)

Organization 3

10. Name of Organization

11.a. City or Town

11.b. State or Province

11.c. Country

12. Nature of Group

Dates of Membership or Dates of Involvement

13.a. From (mm/dd/yyyy)

13.b. To (mm/dd/yyyy)

A-Number ▶ A-

Part 8. General Eligibility and Inadmissibility Grounds (continued)

Answer Item Numbers 14. - 80.b. Choose the answer that you think is correct. If you answer "Yes" to any questions (or if you answer "No," but are unsure of your answer), provide an explanation of the events and circumstances in the space provided in **Part 14. Additional Information**.

14. Have you **EVER** been denied admission to the United States? ☐ Yes ☒ No

15. Have you **EVER** been denied a visa to the United States? ☐ Yes ☒ No

16. Have you **EVER** worked in the United States without authorization? ☐ Yes ☒ No

17. Have you **EVER** violated the terms or conditions of your nonimmigrant status? ☒ Yes ☐ No

18. Are you presently or have you **EVER** been in removal, exclusion, rescission, or deportation proceedings? ☐ Yes ☒ No

19. Have you **EVER** been issued a final order of exclusion, deportation, or removal? ☐ Yes ☒ No

20. Have you **EVER** had a prior final order of exclusion, deportation, or removal reinstated? ☐ Yes ☒ No

21. Have you **EVER** held lawful permanent resident status which was later rescinded? ☐ Yes ☒ No

22. Have you **EVER** been granted voluntary departure by an immigration officer or an immigration judge but failed to depart within the allotted time? ☐ Yes ☒ No

23. Have you **EVER** applied for any kind of relief or protection from removal, exclusion, or deportation? ☐ Yes ☒ No

24.a. Have you **EVER** been a J nonimmigrant exchange visitor who was subject to the two-year foreign residence requirement? ☐ Yes ☒ No

If you answered "Yes" to Item Number 24.a., complete Item Numbers 24.b. - 24.c. If you answered "No" to Item Number 24.a., skip to Item Number 25.

24.b. Have you complied with the foreign residence requirement? ☐ Yes ☐ No

24.c. Have you been granted a waiver or has Department of State issued a favorable waiver recommendation letter for you? ☐ Yes ☐ No

Criminal Acts and Violations

For **Item Numbers 25. - 45.**, you must answer "Yes" to any question that applies to you, even if your records were sealed or otherwise cleared, or even if anyone, including a judge, law enforcement officer, or attorney, told you that you no longer have a record. You must also answer "Yes" to the following questions whether the action or offense occurred here in the United States or anywhere else in the world. If you answer "Yes" to **Item Numbers 25. - 45.**, use the space provided in **Part 14. Additional Information** to provide an explanation that includes why you were arrested, cited, detained, or charged; where you were arrested, cited, detained, or charged; when (date) the event occurred; and the outcome or disposition (for example, no charges filed, charges dismissed, jail, probation, community service).

25. Have you **EVER** been arrested, cited, charged, or detained for any reason by any law enforcement official (including but not limited to any U.S. immigration official or any official of the U.S. armed forces or U.S. Coast Guard)? ☐ Yes ☒ No

26. Have you **EVER** committed a crime of any kind (even if you were not arrested, cited, charged with, or tried for that crime)? ☐ Yes ☒ No

27. Have you **EVER** pled guilty to or been convicted of a crime or offense (even if the violation was subsequently expunged or sealed by a court, or if you were granted a pardon, amnesty, a rehabilitation decree, or other act of clemency)? ☐ Yes ☒ No

NOTE: If you were the beneficiary of a pardon, amnesty, a rehabilitation decree, or other act of clemency, provide documentation of that post-conviction action.

28. Have you **EVER** been ordered punished by a judge or had conditions imposed on you that restrained your liberty (such as a prison sentence, suspended sentence, house arrest, parole, alternative sentencing, drug or alcohol treatment, rehabilitative programs or classes, probation, or community service)? ☐ Yes ☒ No

29. Have you **EVER** been a defendant or the accused in a criminal proceeding (including pre-trial diversion, deferred prosecution, deferred adjudication, or any withheld adjudication)? ☐ Yes ☒ No

30. Have you **EVER** violated (or attempted or conspired to violate) any controlled substance law or regulation of a state, the United States, or a foreign country? ☐ Yes ☒ No

A-Number ▶ A-

Part 8. General Eligibility and Inadmissibility Grounds (continued)

31. Have you **EVER** been convicted of two or more offenses (other than purely political offenses) for which the combined sentences to confinement were five years or more? ☐ Yes ☒ No

32. Have you **EVER** illicitly (illegally) trafficked or benefited from the trafficking of any controlled substances, such as chemicals, illegal drugs, or narcotics? ☐ Yes ☒ No

33. Have you **EVER** knowingly aided, abetted, assisted, conspired, or colluded in the illicit trafficking of any illegal narcotic or other controlled substances? ☐ Yes ☒ No

34. Are you the spouse, son, or daughter of a foreign national who illicitly trafficked or aided (or otherwise abetted, assisted, conspired, or colluded) in the illicit trafficking of a controlled substance, such as chemicals, illegal drugs, or narcotics and you obtained, within the last five years, any financial or other benefit from the illegal activity of your spouse or parent, although you knew or reasonably should have known that the financial or other benefit resulted from the illicit activity of your spouse or parent? ☐ Yes ☒ No

35. Have you **EVER** engaged in prostitution or are you coming to the United States to engage in prostitution? ☐ Yes ☒ No

36. Have you **EVER** directly or indirectly procured (or attempted to procure) or imported prostitutes or persons for the purpose of prostitution? ☐ Yes ☒ No

37. Have you **EVER** received any proceeds or money from prostitution? ☐ Yes ☒ No

38. Do you intend to engage in illegal gambling or any other form of commercialized vice, such as prostitution, bootlegging, or the sale of child pornography, while in the United States? ☐ Yes ☒ No

39. Have you **EVER** exercised immunity (diplomatic or otherwise) to avoid being prosecuted for a criminal offense in the United States? ☐ Yes ☒ No

40. Have you **EVER**, while serving as a foreign government official, been responsible for or directly carried out violations of religious freedoms? ☐ Yes ☒ No

41. Have you **EVER** induced by force, fraud, or coercion (or otherwise been involved in) the trafficking of persons for commercial sex acts? ☐ Yes ☒ No

42. Have you **EVER** trafficked a person into involuntary servitude, peonage, debt bondage, or slavery? Trafficking includes recruiting, harboring, transporting, providing, or obtaining a person for labor or services through the use of force, fraud, or coercion. ☐ Yes ☒ No

43. Have you **EVER** knowingly aided, abetted, assisted, conspired, or colluded with others in trafficking persons for commercial sex acts or involuntary servitude, peonage, debt bondage, or slavery? ☐ Yes ☒ No

44. Are you the spouse, son or daughter of a foreign national who engaged in the trafficking of persons and have received or obtained, within the last five years, any financial or other benefits from the illicit activity of your spouse or your parent, although you knew or reasonably should have known that this benefit resulted from the illicit activity of your spouse or parent? ☐ Yes ☒ No

45. Have you **EVER** engaged in money laundering or have you **EVER** knowingly aided, assisted, conspired, or colluded with others in money laundering or do you seek to enter the United States to engage in such activity? ☐ Yes ☒ No

Security and Related

Do you intend to:

46.a. Engage in any activity that violates or evades any law relating to espionage (including spying) or sabotage in the United States? ☐ Yes ☒ No

46.b. Engage in any activity in the United States that violates or evades any law prohibiting the export from the United States of goods, technology, or sensitive information? ☐ Yes ☒ No

46.c. Engage in any activity whose purpose includes opposing, controlling, or overthrowing the U.S. Government by force, violence, or other unlawful means while in the United States? ☐ Yes ☒ No

46.d. Engage in any activity that could endanger the welfare, safety, or security of the United States? ☐ Yes ☒ No

46.e. Engage in any other unlawful activity? ☐ Yes ☒ No

47. Are you engaged in or, upon your entry into the United States, do you intend to engage in any activity that could have potentially serious adverse foreign policy consequences for the United States? ☐ Yes ☒ No

A-Number ▶ A-

Part 8. General Eligibility and Inadmissibility Grounds (continued)

Have you EVER

48.a. Committed, threatened to commit, attempted to commit, conspired to commit, incited, endorsed, advocated, planned, or prepared any of the following: hijacking, sabotage, kidnapping, political assassination, or use of a weapon or explosive to harm another individual or cause substantial damage to property? ☐ Yes ☒ No

48.b. Participated in, or been a member of, a group or organization that did any of the activities described in Item Number 48.a.? ☐ Yes ☒ No

48.c. Recruited members or asked for money or things of value for a group or organization that did any of the activities described in Item Number 48.a.? ☐ Yes ☒ No

48.d. Provided money, a thing of value, services or labor, or any other assistance or support for any of the activities described in Item Number 48.a.? ☐ Yes ☒ No

48.e. Provided money, a thing of value, services or labor, or any other assistance or support for an individual, group, or organization who did any of the activities described in Item Number 48.a.? ☐ Yes ☒ No

49. Have you **EVER** received any type of military, paramilitary, or weapons training? ☐ Yes ☒ No

50. Do you intend to engage in any of the activities listed in any part of Item Numbers 48.a. - 49.? ☐ Yes ☒ No

NOTE: If you answered "Yes" to any part of **Item Numbers 46.a. - 50.**, explain what you did, including the dates and location of the circumstances, or what you intend to do in the space provided in **Part 14. Additional Information**.

Are you the spouse or child of an individual who EVER

51.a. Committed, threatened to commit, attempted to commit, conspired to commit, incited, endorsed, advocated, planned, or prepared any of the following: hijacking, sabotage, kidnapping, political assassination, or use of a weapon or explosive to harm another individual or cause substantial damage to property? ☐ Yes ☒ No

51.b. Participated in, or been a member or a representative of a group or organization that did any of the activities described in Item Number 51.a.? ☐ Yes ☒ No

51.c. Recruited members, or asked for money or things of value, for a group or organization that did any of the activities described in Item Number 51.a.? ☐ Yes ☒ No

51.d. Provided money, a thing of value, services or labor, or any other assistance or support for any of the activities described in Item Number 51.a.? ☐ Yes ☒ No

51.e. Provided money, a thing of value, services or labor, or any other assistance or support to an individual, group, or organization who did any of the activities described in Item Number 51.a.? ☐ Yes ☒ No

51.f. Received any type of military, paramilitary, or weapons training from a group or organization that did any of the activities described in Item Number 51.a.? ☐ Yes ☒ No

NOTE: If you answered "Yes" to any part of **Item Number 51.**, explain the relationship and what occurred, including the dates and location of the circumstances, in the space provided in **Part 14. Additional Information**.

52. Have you **EVER** assisted or participated in selling, providing, or transporting weapons to any person who, to your knowledge, used them against another person? ☐ Yes ☒ No

53. Have you **EVER** worked, volunteered, or otherwise served in any prison, jail, prison camp, detention facility, labor camp, or any other situation that involved detaining persons? ☐ Yes ☒ No

54. Have you **EVER** been a member of, assisted, or participated in any group, unit, or organization of any kind in which you or other persons used any type of weapon against any person or threatened to do so? ☐ Yes ☒ No

55. Have you **EVER** served in, been a member of, assisted, or participated in any military unit, paramilitary unit, police unit, self-defense unit, vigilante unit, rebel group, guerilla group, militia, insurgent organization, or any other armed group? ☐ Yes ☒ No

56. Have you **EVER** been a member of, or in any way affiliated with the Communist Party or any other totalitarian party (in the United States or abroad)? ☐ Yes ☒ No

57. During the period from March 23, 1933 to May 8, 1945, did you ever order, incite, assist, or otherwise participate in the persecution of any person because of race, religion, national origin, or political opinion, in association with either the Nazi government of Germany or any organization or government associated or allied with the Nazi government of Germany? ☐ Yes ☒ No

A-Number ▶ A-

Part 8. General Eligibility and Inadmissibility Grounds (continued)

Have you EVER ordered, incited, called for, committed, assisted, helped with, or otherwise participated in any of the following:

58.a. Acts involving torture or genocide? ☐ Yes ☒ No

58.b. Killing any person? ☐ Yes ☒ No

58.c. Intentionally and severely injuring any person? ☐ Yes ☒ No

58.d. Engaging in any kind of sexual contact or relations with any person who did not consent or was unable to consent, or was being forced or threatened? ☐ Yes ☒ No

58.e. Limiting or denying any person's ability to exercise religious beliefs? ☐ Yes ☒ No

59. Have you EVER recruited, enlisted, conscripted, or used any person under 15 years of age to serve in or help an armed force or group? ☐ Yes ☒ No

60. Have you EVER used any person under 15 years of age to take part in hostilities, or to help or provide services to people in combat? ☐ Yes ☒ No

NOTE: If you answered "Yes" to any part of **Item Numbers 52. - 60.**, explain what occurred, including the dates and location of the circumstances, in the space provided in **Part 14. Additional Information.**

Public Assistance

61. Have you received public assistance in the United States from any source, including the U.S. Government or any state, county, city, or municipality (other than emergency medical treatment)? ☐ Yes ☒ No

62. Are you likely to receive public assistance in the future in the United States from any source, including the U.S. Government or any state, county, city, or municipality (other than emergency medical treatment)? ☐ Yes ☒ No

Illegal Entries and Other Immigration Violations

63.a. Have you EVER failed or refused to attend or to remain in attendance at any removal proceeding filed against you on or after April 1, 1997? ☐ Yes ☒ No

63.b. If your answer to **Item Number 63.a.** is "Yes," do you believe you had reasonable cause? ☐ Yes ☒ No

63.c. If your answer to **Item Number 63.b.** is "Yes," attach a written statement explaining why you had reasonable cause.

64. Have you EVER submitted fraudulent or counterfeit documentation to any U.S. Government official to obtain or attempt to obtain any immigration benefit, including a visa or entry into the United States? ☐ Yes ☒ No

65. Have you EVER lied about, concealed, or misrepresented any information on an application or petition to obtain a visa, other documentation required for entry into the United States, admission to the United States, or any other kind of immigration benefit? ☐ Yes ☒ No

66. Have you EVER falsely claimed to be a U.S. citizen (in writing or any other way)? ☐ Yes ☒ No

67. Have you EVER been a stowaway on a vessel or aircraft arriving in the United States? ☐ Yes ☒ No

68. Have you EVER knowingly encouraged, induced, assisted, abetted, or aided any foreign national to enter or to try to enter the United States illegally (alien smuggling)? ☐ Yes ☒ No

69. Are you under a final order of civil penalty for violating INA section 274C for use of fraudulent documents? ☐ Yes ☒ No

Removal, Unlawful Presence, or Illegal Reentry After Previous Immigration Violations

70. Have you EVER been excluded, deported, or removed from the United States or have you ever departed the United States on your own after having been ordered excluded, deported, or removed from the United States? ☐ Yes ☒ No

71. Have you EVER entered the United States without being inspected and admitted or paroled? ☐ Yes ☒ No

Since April 1, 1997, have you been unlawfully present in the United States:

72.a. For more than 180 days but less than a year, and then departed the United States? ☐ Yes ☒ No

72.b. For one year or more and then departed the United States? ☐ Yes ☒ No

NOTE: You were unlawfully present in the United States if you entered the United States without being inspected and admitted or inspected and paroled, or if you legally entered the United States but you stayed longer than permitted.

A-Number ▶ A-

Part 8. General Eligibility and Inadmissibility Grounds (continued)

Since April 1, 1997, have you EVER reentered or attempted to reenter the United States without being inspected and admitted or paroled after:

73.a. Having been unlawfully present in the United States for more than one year in the aggregate? ☐ Yes ☒ No

73.b. Having been deported, excluded, or removed from the United States? ☐ Yes ☒ No

Miscellaneous Conduct

74. Do you plan to practice polygamy in the United States? ☐ Yes ☒ No

75. Are you accompanying another foreign national who requires your protection or guardianship but who is inadmissible after being certified by a medical officer as being helpless from sickness, physical or mental disability, or infancy, as described in INA section 212(c)? ☐ Yes ☒ No

76. Have you EVER assisted in detaining, retaining, or withholding custody of a U.S. citizen child outside the United States from a U.S. citizen who has been granted custody of the child? ☐ Yes ☒ No

77. Have you EVER voted in violation of any Federal, state, or local constitutional provision, statute, ordinance, or regulation in the United States? ☐ Yes ☒ No

78. Have you EVER renounced U.S. citizenship to avoid being taxed by the United States? ☐ Yes ☒ No

Have you EVER:

79.a. Applied for exemption or discharge from training or service in the U.S. armed forces or in the U.S. National Security Training Corps on the ground that you are a foreign national? ☐ Yes ☒ No

79.b. Been relieved or discharged from such training or service on the ground that you are a foreign national? ☐ Yes ☒ No

79.c. Been convicted of desertion from the U.S. armed forces? ☐ Yes ☒ No

80.a. Have you EVER left or remained outside the United States to avoid or evade training or service in the U.S. armed forces in time of war or a period declared by the President to be a national emergency? ☐ Yes ☒ No

80.b. If your answer to Item Number 80.a. is "Yes," what was your nationality or immigration status immediately before you left (for example, U.S. citizen or national, lawful permanent resident, nonimmigrant, parolee, present without admission or parole, or any other status)?

Part 9. Accommodations for Individuals With Disabilities and/or Impairments

NOTE: Read the information in the Form I-485 Instructions before completing this part.

1. Are you requesting an accommodation because of your disabilities and/or impairments? ☐ Yes ☒ No

If you answered "Yes" to Item Number 1., select any applicable box in Item Numbers 2.a. - 2.c. and provide an answer.

2.a. ☐ I am deaf or hard of hearing and request the following accommodation. (If you are requesting a sign-language interpreter, indicate for which language (for example, American Sign Language).)

2.b. ☐ I am blind or have low vision and request the following accommodation.

2.c. ☐ I have another type of disability and/or impairment. (Describe the nature of your disability and/or impairment and the accommodation you are requesting.)

A-Number ▶ A-

Part 10. Applicant's Statement, Contact Information, Declaration, Certification, and Signature

NOTE: Read the **Penalties** section of the Form I-485 Instructions before completing this part. You must file Form I-485 while in the United States.

Applicant's Statement

NOTE: Select the box for either **Item Number 1.a.** or **1.b.** If applicable, select the box for **Item Number 2.**

1.a. [X] I can read and understand English, and I have read and understand every question and instruction on this application and my answer to every question.

1.b. [ ] The interpreter named in Part 11. read to me every question and instruction on this application and my answer to every question in

a language in which I am fluent, and I understood everything.

2. [X] At my request, the preparer named in Part 12.,

Christopher A. Reed

prepared this application for me based only upon information I provided or authorized.

Applicant's Contact Information

3. Applicant's Daytime Telephone Number

(323) 404-2220

4. Applicant's Mobile Telephone Number (if any)

[redacted]

5. Applicant's Email Address (if any)

[redacted]

Applicant's Declaration and Certification

Copies of any documents I have submitted are exact photocopies of unaltered, original documents, and I understand that USCIS may require that I submit original documents to USCIS at a later date. Furthermore, I authorize the release of any information from any and all of my records that USCIS may need to determine my eligibility for the immigration benefit that I seek.

I understand that if I am a male who is 18 to 26 years of age, submitting this application will automatically register me with the Selective Service System as required by the Military Selective Service Act.

I furthermore authorize release of information contained in this application, in supporting documents, and in my USCIS records, to other entities and persons where necessary for the administration and enforcement of U.S. immigration law.

I understand that USCIS may require me to appear for an appointment to take my biometrics (fingerprints, photograph, and/or signature) and, at that time, if I am required to provide biometrics, I will be required to sign an oath reaffirming that:

1) I reviewed and understood all of the information contained in, and submitted with, my application; and

2) All of this information was complete, true, and correct at the time of filing.

I certify, under penalty of perjury, that all of the information in my application and any document submitted with it were provided or authorized by me, that I reviewed and understand all of the information contained in, and submitted with, my application and that all of this information is complete, true, and correct.

Applicant's Signature

6.a. Applicant's Signature (sign in ink)

[redacted]

6.b. Date 7/19/18

NOTE TO ALL APPLICANTS: If you do not completely fill out this application or fail to submit required documents listed in the Instructions, USCIS may deny your application.

Part 11. Interpreter's Contact Information, Certification, and Signature

Provide the following information about the interpreter.

Interpreter's Full Name

1.a. Interpreter's Family Name (Last Name)

1.b. Interpreter's Given Name (First Name)

2. Interpreter's Business or Organization Name (if any)

A-Number ▶ A-

Part 11. Interpreter's Contact Information, Certification, and Signature (continued)

Interpreter's Mailing Address

3.a. Street Number and Name

3.b. ☐ Apt. ☐ Ste. ☐ Flr.

3.c. City or Town

3.d. State 3.e. ZIP Code

3.f. Province

3.g. Postal Code

3.h. Country

Interpreter's Contact Information

4. Interpreter's Daytime Telephone Number

5. Interpreter's Mobile Telephone Number (if any)

6. Interpreter's Email Address (if any)

Interpreter's Certification

I certify, under penalty of perjury, that:

I am fluent in English and ______, which is the same language specified in Part 10., Item Number 1.b., and I have read to this applicant in the identified language every question and instruction on this application and his or her answer to every question. The applicant informed me that he or she understands every instruction, question, and answer on the application, including the Applicant's Declaration and Certification, and has verified the accuracy of every answer.

Interpreter's Signature

7.a. Interpreter's Signature (sign in ink)

7.b. Date of Signature (mm/dd/yyyy)

Part 12. Contact Information, Declaration, and Signature of the Person Preparing this Application, if Other Than the Applicant

Provide the following information about the preparer.

Preparer's Full Name

1.a. Preparer's Family Name (Last Name)
Reed

1.b. Preparer's Given Name (First Name)
Christopher

2. Preparer's Business or Organization Name (if any)
Law Offices of Brian D. Lerner, APC

Preparer's Mailing Address

3.a. Street Number and Name 3233 E. Broadway

3.b. ☐ Apt. ☐ Ste. ☐ Flr.

3.c. City or Town Long Beach

3.d. State CA 3.e. ZIP Code 90803

3.f. Province

3.g. Postal Code

3.h. Country
USA

Preparer's Contact Information

4. Preparer's Daytime Telephone Number
(562) 495-0554

5. Preparer's Mobile Telephone Number (if any)

6. Preparer's Email Address (if any)
creed@eimmigration.org

A-Number ▶ A-

Part 12. Contact Information, Declaration, and Signature of the Person Preparing this Application, if Other Than the Applicant (continued)

Preparer's Statement

7.a. ☐ I am not an attorney or accredited representative but have prepared this application on behalf of the applicant and with the applicant's consent.

7.b. ☒ I am an attorney or accredited representative and my representation of the applicant in this case ☒ extends ☐ does not extend beyond the preparation of this application.

NOTE: If you are an attorney or accredited representative, you may be obliged to submit a completed Form G-28, Notice of Entry of Appearance as Attorney or Accredited Representative, with this application.

Preparer's Certification

By my signature, I certify, under penalty of perjury, that I prepared this application at the request of the applicant. The applicant then reviewed this completed application and informed me that he or she understands all of the information contained in, and submitted with, his or her application, including the **Applicant's Declaration and Certification**, and that all of this information is complete, true, and correct. I completed this application based only on information that the applicant provided to me or authorized me to obtain or use.

Preparer's Signature

8.a. Preparer's Signature (sign in ink)

8.b. Date of Signature (mm/dd/yyyy) 7/23/18

NOTE: Do not complete Part 13, until the USCIS Officer instructs you to do so at the interview.

Part 13. Signature at Interview

I swear (affirm) and certify under penalty of perjury under the laws of the United States of America that I know that the contents of this Form I-485, Application to Register Permanent Residence or Adjust Status, subscribed by me, including the corrections made to this application, numbered ____ through ____, are complete, true, and correct. All additional pages submitted by me with this Form I-485, on numbered pages ____ through ____ are complete, true, and correct. All documents submitted at this interview were provided by me and are complete, true, and correct.

Subscribed to and sworn to (affirmed) before me

USCIS Officer's Printed Name or Stamp

Date of Signature (mm/dd/yyyy)

Applicant's Signature (sign in ink)

USCIS Officer's Signature (sign in ink)

A-Number ▶ A-

Part 14. Additional Information

If you need extra space to provide any additional information within this application, use the space below. If you need more space than what is provided, you may make copies of this page to complete and file with this application or attach a separate sheet of paper. Type or print your name and A-Number (if any) at the top of each sheet; indicate the **Page Number**, **Part Number**, and **Item Number** to which your answer refers; and sign and date each sheet.

1.a. Family Name (Last Name) [redacted]

1.b. Given Name (First Name) [redacted]

1.c. Middle Name [redacted]

2. A-Number (if any) ▶ A-

3.a. Page Number 3.b. Part Number 3.c. Item Number

3.d.

4.a. Page Number 4.b. Part Number 4.c. Item Number

4.d.

5.a. Page Number 5.b. Part Number 5.c. Item Number

5.d.

6.a. Page Number 6.b. Part Number 6.c. Item Number

6.d.

7.a. Page Number 7.b. Part Number 7.c. Item Number

7.d.

Addendum

[redacted] Form: I-485 (Page 1)

Part 3. Additional Residential History:

From: 06/15/2014 through 08/01/2016
1521 Rose Court
West Covina, CA 91791 USA

From: 02/01/2013 through 06/15/2014
2648 Erica Avenue
West Covina, CA 91792 USA

Part 8 Number 17.:
I have lived in the United States under Unlawful Status for more than one year

Application For Employment Authorization
Department of Homeland Security
U.S. Citizenship and Immigration Services

USCIS
Form I-765
OMB No. 1615-0040
Expires 02/28/2018

For USCIS Use Only	Fee Stamp	Action Block	Initial Receipt	Resubmitted
			Relocated	
			Received	Sent
			Completed	
Application Approved	Application Denied - Failed to establish:		Approved	Denied
Authorization/Extension Valid From ____	Eligibility under 8 CFR 274a.12 (a) or (c)	Economic necessity under 8 CFR 274a.12(c)(14), (18) and 8 CFR 214.2(f)		
Authorization/Extension Valid To ____			AR	
Subject to the following conditions: ____	Applicant is filing under section 274a.12 ____			

▶ START HERE - Type or print in black ink.

I am applying for:

☒ Permission to accept employment.

☐ Replacement (of lost employment authorization document).

☐ Renewal of my permission to accept employment (attach a copy of your previous employment authorization document).

1. Full Name

Family Name	First Name	Middle Name
[redacted]	[redacted]	[redacted]

2. Other Names Used (include Maiden Name)

Family Name	First Name	Middle Name

3. U.S. Mailing Address

Street Number and Name	Apt. Number
[redacted]	5C

Town or City	State	ZIP Code
[redacted]	CA	91745

4. Country of Citizenship or Nationality

[redacted]

5. Place of Birth

Town or City	State/Province	Country
[redacted]	[redacted]	Philippines

6. Date of Birth (mm/dd/yyyy) 01/04/1980

7. Gender ☐ Male ☒ Female

8. Marital Status

☐ Single ☒ Married ☐ Divorced ☐ Widowed

9.a. Has the Social Security Administration (SSA) ever officially issued a Social Security card to you?

☐ Yes ☒ No

NOTE: If you answered "Yes" to Item Number 9.a., provide the information requested in Item Number 9.b.

9.b. Provide your Social Security number (SSN) (if known).

▶

10. Do you want the SSA to issue you a Social Security card? (You must also answer "Yes" to Item Number 11., Consent for Disclosure, to receive a card.)

☒ Yes ☐ No

NOTE: If you answered "No" to Item Number 10., skip to Item Number 14. If you answered "Yes" to Item Number 10., you must also answer "Yes" to Item Number 11.

11. Consent for Disclosure: I authorize disclosure of information from this application to the SSA as required for the purpose of assigning me an SSN and issuing me a Social Security card.

☒ Yes ☐ No

NOTE: If you answered "Yes" to Item Numbers 10. - 11., provide the information requested in Item Numbers 12.a. - 13.b.

Father's Name

12.a. Family Name (Last Name) [redacted]

Mother's Name (Provide your mother's birth name.)

13.a. Family Name (Last Name) [redacted]

13.b. Given Name (First Name) Clarita

14. **Alien Registration Number (A-Number) or Form I-94 Number** (if any)

[redacted]

15. **Have you ever before applied for employment authorization from USCIS?**

☐ Yes (Complete the following questions.)

Which USCIS Office? Dates

Results (Granted or Denied - attach all documentation)

☒ No (Proceed to Item Number 16.)

16. **Date of Your Last Arrival or Entry Into the U.S., On or About** (mm/dd/yyyy)

03/30/2005

17. **Place of Your Last Arrival or Entry Into the U.S.**

Los Angeles, CA

18. **Status at Last Entry** (B-2 Visitor, F-1 Student, No Lawful Status, etc.)

B-2

19. **Current Immigration Status** (Visitor, Student, etc.)

Unlawful Status

20. **Eligibility Category.** Go to the Who May File Form I-765? section of the Instructions. In the space below, place the letter and number of the eligibility category you selected from the instructions. For example, (a)(8), (c)(17)(iii), etc.

(c) (9) ( )

21. **(c)(3)(C) Eligibility Category.** If you entered the eligibility category (c)(3)(C) in **Item Number 20.** above, list your degree, your employer's name as listed in E-Verify, and your employer's E-Verify Company Identification Number or a valid E-Verify Client Company Identification Number in the space below.

Degree Employer's Name as listed in E-Verify

Employer's E-Verify Company Identification Number or a Valid E-Verify Client Company Identification Number

22. **(c)(26) Eligibility Category.** If you entered the eligibility category (c)(26) in **Item Number 20.** above, please provide the receipt number of your H-1B principal spouse's most recent Form I-797 Notice of Approval for Form I-129.

23. **(c)(35) and (c)(36) Eligibility Category**

a. If you entered the eligibility category (c)(35) or (c)(36) in **Item Number 20.** above, please provide the receipt number of the Form I-140 beneficiary's Form I-797 Notice of Approval for Form I-140.

b. Have you **EVER** been arrested for and/or convicted of any crime? ☐ Yes ☐ No

NOTE: If you answered "Yes" to **Item Number 23.b.**, refer to **Item Number 5.**, **Item H.** or **Item L.** in the **Who May File Form I-765** section of these Instructions for information about providing court dispositions.

Certification

I certify, under penalty of perjury, that the foregoing is true and correct. Furthermore, I authorize the release of any information that U.S. Citizenship and Immigration Services needs to determine eligibility for the benefit I am seeking. I have read the **Who May File Form I-765** section of the Instructions and have identified the appropriate eligibility category in **Item Number 20.**

Applicant's Signature

Date of Signature (mm/dd/yyyy) 7/19/18

Telephone Number

(323) 404-2220

Signature of Person Preparing Form, If Other Than Applicant

I declare that this document was prepared by me at the request of the applicant and is based on all information of which I have any knowledge.

Preparer's Signature

Date of Signature (mm/dd/yyyy) 7/23/18

Printed Name

Christopher A. Reed

Address

Law Offices of Brian D. Lerner, APC
3233 E. Broadway

Affidavit of Support Under Section 213A of the INA

Department of Homeland Security
U.S. Citizenship and Immigration Services

USCIS
Form I-864
OMB No. 1615-0075
Expires 03/31/2020

For USCIS Use Only	Affidavit of Support Submitter	Section 213A Review	Number of Support Affidavits in File
	☐ Petitioner ☐ 1st Joint Sponsor ☐ 2nd Joint Sponsor ☐ Substitute Sponsor ☐ 5% Owner	☐ MEETS requirements ☐ DOES NOT MEET requirements Reviewed By: Office Date (mm/dd/yyyy)	☐ 1 ☐ 2 Remarks

To be completed by an attorney or accredited representative (if any).	☒ Select this box if Form G-28 or G-28I is attached.	Attorney State Bar Number (if applicable) 235438	Attorney or Accredited Representative USCIS Online Account Number (if any)

► START HERE - Type or print in black ink.

Part 1. Basis For Filing Affidavit of Support

1. I, Daniel Glenn DEUEL am the sponsor submitting this affidavit of support because (Select only one box):

1.a. ☒ I am the petitioner. I filed or am filing for the immigration of my relative.

1.b. ☐ I filed an alien worker petition on behalf of the intending immigrant, who is related to me as my

1.c. ☐ I have an ownership interest of at least 5 percent in which filed an alien worker petition on behalf of the intending immigrant, who is related to me as my

1.d. ☐ I am the only joint sponsor.

1.e. ☐ I am the ☐ first ☐ second of two joint sponsors.

1.f. ☐ The original petitioner is deceased. I am the substitute sponsor. I am the intending immigrant's

NOTE: If you are filing this form as a sponsor, you must include proof of your U.S. citizenship, U.S. national status, or lawful permanent resident status.

Part 2. Information About the Principal Immigrant

1.a. Family Name (Last Name) [redacted]

1.b. Given Name (First Name) [redacted]

1.c. Middle Name [redacted]

Mailing Address

2.a. In Care Of Name

2.b. Street Number and Name [redacted]

2.c. ☒ Apt. ☐ Ste. ☐ Flr. 5C

2.d. City or Town [redacted]

2.e. State CA 2.f. ZIP Code [redacted]

2.g. Province

2.h. Postal Code

2.i. Country USA

Other Information

3. Country of Citizenship or Nationality Philippines

4. Date of Birth (mm/dd/yyyy) 01/04/1980

5. Alien Registration Number (A-Number) (if any) ► A-

6. USCIS Online Account Number (if any) ►

7. Daytime Telephone Number [redacted]

Part 3. Information About the Immigrants You Are Sponsoring

1. I am sponsoring the principal immigrant named in Part 2.

   [X] Yes [ ] No (Applicable only if you are sponsoring family members in Part 3. as the second joint sponsor or if you are sponsoring family members who are immigrating more than six months after the principal immigrant)

2. [ ] I am sponsoring the following family members immigrating at the same time or within six months of the principal immigrant named in Part 2. (Do not include any relative listed on a separate visa petition.)

3. [ ] I am sponsoring the following family members who are immigrating more than six months after the principal immigrant.

Family Member 1

4.a. Family Name (Last Name)

4.b. Given Name (First Name)

4.c. Middle Name

5. Relationship to Principal Immigrant

6. Date of Birth (mm/dd/yyyy)

7. Alien Registration Number (A-Number) (if any)
   ► A-

8. USCIS Online Account Number (if any)
   ►

Family Member 2

9.a. Family Name (Last Name)

9.b. Given Name (First Name)

9.c. Middle Name

10. Relationship to Principal Immigrant

11. Date of Birth (mm/dd/yyyy)

12. Alien Registration Number (A-Number) (if any)
   ► A-

13. USCIS Online Account Number (if any)
   ►

Family Member 3

14.a. Family Name (Last Name)

14.b. Given Name (First Name)

14.c. Middle Name

15. Relationship to Principal Immigrant

16. Date of Birth (mm/dd/yyyy)

17. Alien Registration Number (A-Number) (if any)
   ► A-

18. USCIS Online Account Number (if any)
   ►

Family Member 4

19.a. Family Name (Last Name)

19.b. Given Name (First Name)

19.c. Middle Name

20. Relationship to Principal Immigrant

21. Date of Birth (mm/dd/yyyy)

22. Alien Registration Number (A-Number) (if any)
   ► A-

23. USCIS Online Account Number (if any)
   ►

Family Member 5

24.a. Family Name (Last Name)

24.b. Given Name (First Name)

24.c. Middle Name

25. Relationship to Principal Immigrant

26. Date of Birth (mm/dd/yyyy)

27. Alien Registration Number (A-Number) (if any)
   ► A-

28. USCIS Online Account Number (if any)
   ►

Part 3. Information About the Immigrants You Are Sponsoring (continued)

29. Enter the total number of immigrants you are sponsoring on this affidavit which includes the principal immigrant listed in Part 2., any immigrants listed in Part 3., Item Numbers 1. - 28. and (if applicable), any immigrants listed for these questions in Part 11. Additional Information. Do not count the principal immigrant if you are only sponsoring family members entering more than 6 months after the principal immigrant. 1

Part 4. Information About You (Sponsor)

Sponsor's Full Name

1.a. Family Name (Last Name) DEUEL

1.b. Given Name (First Name) Daniel

1.c. Middle Name Glenn

Sponsor's Mailing Address

2.a. In Care Of Name

2.b. Street Number and Name 15727 Tetley Street

2.c. [X] Apt. [ ] Ste. [ ] Flr. 5C

2.d. City or Town Hacienda Heights

2.e. State CA 2.f. ZIP Code 917 4

2.g. Province

2.h. Postal Code

2.i. Country USA

3. Is your current mailing address the same as your physical address? [X] Yes [ ] No

If you answered "No" to Item Number 3., provide your physical address in Item Numbers 4.a. - 4.h.

Sponsor's Physical Address

4.a. Street Number and Name

4.b. [ ] Apt. [ ] Ste. [ ] Flr.

4.c. City or Town

4.d. State 4.e. ZIP Code

4.f. Province

4.g. Postal Code

4.h. Country

Other Information

5. Country of Domicile USA

6. Date of Birth (mm/dd/yyyy) 04/05/1967

7. City or Town of Birth Binghamton

8. State or Province of Birth New York

9. Country of Birth USA

10. U.S. Social Security Number (Required) ▶ [redacted]

Citizenship or Residency

11.a. [X] I am a U.S. citizen.

11.b. [ ] I am a U.S. national.

11.c. [ ] I am a lawful permanent resident.

12. Sponsor's A-Number (if any) ▶ A-

13. Sponsor's USCIS Online Account Number (if any) ▶

Military Service (To be completed by petitioner sponsors only.)

14. I am currently on active duty in the U.S. Armed Forces or U.S. Coast Guard. [ ] Yes [X] No

For USCIS Use Only

Part 5. Sponsor's Household Size

NOTE: Do not count any member of your household more than once.

Persons you are sponsoring in this affidavit:

1. Provide the number you entered in Part 3., Item Number 29. [1]

Persons NOT sponsored in this affidavit:

2. Yourself. [1]
3. If you are currently married, enter "1" for your spouse. [ ]
4. If you have dependent children, enter the number here. [ ]
5. If you have any other dependents, enter the number here. [ ]
6. If you have sponsored any other persons on Form I-864 or Form I-864EZ who are now lawful permanent residents, enter the number here. [ ]
7. OPTIONAL: If you have siblings, parents, or adult children with the same principal residence who are combining their income with yours by submitting Form I-864A, enter the number here. [ ]
8. Add together Part 5., Item Numbers 1. - 7. and enter the number here.

Household Size: [2]

Part 6. Sponsor's Employment and Income

I am currently:

1. [X] Employed as a/an [ ]
2. Name of Employer 1 [Unemployed]
3. Name of Employer 2 (if applicable) [ ]
4. [ ] Self-Employed as a/an (Occupation) [ ]
5. [ ] Retired Since (mm/dd/yyyy) [ ]
6. [ ] Unemployed Since (mm/dd/yyyy) [ ]
7. My current individual annual income is: $ [2000]

Income you are using from any other person who was counted in your household size, including, in certain conditions, the intending immigrant. (See Form I-864 Instructions.) Please indicate name, relationship, and income.

Person 1

8. Name [ ]
9. Relationship [ ]
10. Current Income $ [0]

Person 2

11. Name [ ]
12. Relationship [ ]
13. Current Income $ [0]

Person 3

14. Name [ ]
15. Relationship [ ]
16. Current Income $ [0]

Person 4

17. Name [ ]
18. Relationship [ ]
19. Current Income $ [0]

For USCIS Use Only	Household Size	Poverty Guideline	Remarks
	☐ 1 ☐ 2 ☐ 3 ☐ 4 ☐ 5 ☐ 6 ☐ 7 ☐ 8 ☐ 9 ☐ Other ______	Year 20____ Poverty Line $______	

Part 6. Sponsor's Employment and Income (continued)

20. My Current Annual Household Income (Total all lines from Part 6. Item Numbers 7., 10., 13., 16., and 19., the total will be compared to Federal Poverty Guidelines on Form I-864P.) $ 2000

21. [X] The people listed in Item Numbers 8., 11., 14., and 17. have completed Form I-864A. I am filing along with this affidavit all necessary Form I-864As completed by these people.

22. ☐ One or more of the people listed in Item Numbers 8., 11., 14., and 17. do not need to complete Form I-864A because he or she is the intending immigrant and has no accompanying dependents.

Name ______

Federal Income Tax Return Information

23.a. Have you filed a Federal income tax return for each of the three most recent tax years? [X] Yes ☐ No

NOTE: You MUST attach a photocopy or transcript of your Federal income tax return for only the most recent tax year.

23.b. ☐ (Optional) I have attached photocopies or transcripts of my Federal income tax returns for my second and third most recent tax years.

My total income (adjusted gross income on Internal Revenue Service (IRS) Form 1040EZ) as reported on my Federal income tax returns for the most recent three years was:

	Tax Year	Total Income
24.a. Most Recent	2017	$ 2,686.00
24.b. 2nd Most Recent	2016	$ 1,188.00
24.c. 3rd Most Recent	2015	$ 1,252.00

25. ☐ I was not required to file a Federal income tax return as my income was below the IRS required level and I have attached evidence to support this.

Part 7. Use of Assets to Supplement Income (Optional)

If your income, or the total income for you and your household, from Part 6., Item Numbers 20. or 24.a. - 24.c., exceeds the Federal Poverty Guidelines for your household size, YOU ARE NOT REQUIRED to complete this Part 7. Skip to Part 8.

Your Assets (Optional)

1. Enter the balance of all savings and checking accounts. $______

2. Enter the net cash value of real estate holdings. (Net value means current assessed value minus mortgage debt.) $______

3. Enter the net cash value of all stocks, bonds, certificates of deposit, and any other assets not already included in Item Number 1. or Item Number 2. $______

4. Add together Item Numbers 1. - 3. and enter the number here. TOTAL: $______

Assets from Form I-864A, Part 4., Item Number 3.d., for:

5.a. Name of Relative ______

5.b. Your household member's assets from Form I-864A (optional). $______

Assets of the principal sponsored immigrant (optional)

The principal sponsored immigrant is the person listed in Part 2., Item Numbers 1.a. - 1.c. Only include the assets if the principal immigrant is being sponsored by this affidavit of support.

6. Enter the balance of the principal immigrant's savings and checking accounts. $______

7. Enter the net cash value of all the principal immigrant's real estate holdings. (Net value means investment value minus mortgage debt.) $______

8. Enter the current cash value of the principal immigrant's stocks, bonds, certificates of deposit, and other assets not included in Item Number 6. or Item Number 7. $______

For USCIS Use Only	Household Size	Poverty Guideline	Sponsor's Household Income (Page 3, Line 10)	Remarks
	☐ 1 ☐ 2 ☐ 3 ☐ 4 ☐ 5 ☐ 6	Year: 20____	$____________	
	☐ 7 ☐ 8 ☐ 9 ☐ Other______	Poverty Line: $____________	*The total value of all assets, line 10, must equal 5 times (3 times for spouses and children of USCs, or 1 time for orphans to be formally adopted in the U.S.) the difference between the poverty guidelines and the sponsor's household income, line 10.*	

Part 7. Use of Assets to Supplement Income (Optional) (continued)

9. Add together Item Numbers 6. - 8. and enter the number here.
$ [ ]

Total Value of Assets

10. Add together Item Numbers 4., 5.b., and 9. and enter the number here.
TOTAL: $ [ ]

Part 8. Sponsor's Contract, Statement, Contact Information, Declaration, Certification, and Signature

NOTE: Read the Penalties section of the Form I-864 Instructions before completing this part.

Sponsor's Contract

Please note that, by signing this Form I-864, you agree to assume certain specific obligations under the Immigration and Nationality Act (INA) and other Federal laws. The following paragraphs describe those obligations. Please read the following information carefully before you sign Form I-864. If you do not understand the obligations, you may wish to consult an attorney or accredited representative.

What is the Legal Effect of My Signing Form I-864?

If you sign Form I-864 on behalf of any person (called the intending immigrant) who is applying for an immigrant visa or for adjustment of status to a lawful permanent resident, and that intending immigrant submits Form I-864 to the U.S. Government with his or her application for an immigrant visa or adjustment of status, under INA section 213A, these actions create a contract between you and the U.S. Government. The intending immigrant becoming a lawful permanent resident is the consideration for the contract.

Under this contract, you agree that, in deciding whether the intending immigrant can establish that he or she is not inadmissible to the United States as a person likely to become a public charge, the U.S. Government can consider your income and assets as available for the support of the intending immigrant.

What If I Choose Not to Sign Form I-864?

The U.S. Government cannot make you sign Form I-864 if you do not want to do so. But if you do not sign Form I-864, the intending immigrant may not become a lawful permanent resident in the United States.

What Does Signing Form I-864 Require Me To Do?

If an intending immigrant becomes a lawful permanent resident in the United States based on a Form I-864 that you have signed, then, until your obligations under Form I-864 terminate, you must:

A. Provide the intending immigrant any support necessary to maintain him or her at an income that is at least 125 percent of the Federal Poverty Guidelines for his or her household size (100 percent if you are the petitioning sponsor and are on active duty in the U.S. Armed Forces or U.S. Coast Guard, and the person is your husband, wife, or unmarried child under 21 years of age); and

B. Notify U.S. Citizenship and Immigration Services (USCIS) of any change in your address, within 30 days of the change, by filing Form I-865.

What Other Consequences Are There?

If an intending immigrant becomes a lawful permanent resident in the United States based on a Form I-864 that you have signed, then, until your obligations under Form I-864 terminate, the U.S. Government may consider (deem) your income and assets as available to that person, in determining whether he or she is eligible for certain Federal means-tested public benefits and also for state or local means-tested public benefits, if the state or local government's rules provide for consideration (deeming) of your income and assets as available to the person.

This provision does not apply to public benefits specified in section 403(c) of the Welfare Reform Act such as emergency Medicaid, short-term, non-cash emergency relief; services provided under the National School Lunch and Child Nutrition Acts; immunizations and testing and treatment for communicable diseases; and means-tested programs under the Elementary and Secondary Education Act.

What If I Do Not Fulfill My Obligations?

If you do not provide sufficient support to the person who becomes a lawful permanent resident based on a Form I-864 that you signed, that person may sue you for this support

Part 8. Sponsor's Contract, Statement, Contact Information, Declaration, Certification, and Signature (continued)

If a Federal, state, local, or private agency provided any covered means-tested public benefit to the person who becomes a lawful permanent resident based on a Form I-864 that you signed, the agency may ask you to reimburse them for the amount of the benefits they provided. If you do not make the reimbursement, the agency may sue you for the amount that the agency believes you owe.

If you are sued, and the court enters a judgment against you, the person or agency that sued you may use any legally permitted procedures for enforcing or collecting the judgment. You may also be required to pay the costs of collection, including attorney fees.

If you do not file a properly completed Form I-865 within 30 days of any change of address, USCIS may impose a civil fine for your failing to do so.

When Will These Obligations End?

Your obligations under a Form I-864 that you signed will end if the person who becomes a lawful permanent resident based on that affidavit:

A. Becomes a U.S. citizen;

B. Has worked, or can receive credit for, 40 quarters of coverage under the Social Security Act;

C. No longer has lawful permanent resident status and has departed the United States;

D. Is subject to removal, but applies for and obtains, in removal proceedings, a new grant of adjustment of status, based on a new affidavit of support, if one is required; or

E. Dies.

NOTE: Divorce does not terminate your obligations under Form I-864.

Your obligations under a Form I-864 that you signed also end if you die. Therefore, if you die, your estate is not required to take responsibility for the person's support after your death. However, your estate may owe any support that you accumulated before you died.

Sponsor's Statement

NOTE: Select the box for either Item Number 1.a. or 1.b. If applicable, select the box for Item Number 2.

1.a. [x] I can read and understand English, and I have read and understand every question and instruction on this affidavit and my answer to every question.

1.b. [ ] The interpreter named in Part 9. read to me every question and instruction on this affidavit and my answer to every question in

a language in which I am fluent, and I understood everything.

2. [x] At my request, the preparer named in Part 10.

Christopher A Reed

prepared this affidavit for me based only upon information I provided or authorized.

Sponsor's Contact Information

3. Sponsor's Daytime Telephone Number

[redacted]

4. Sponsor's Mobile Telephone Number (if any)

[redacted]

5. Sponsor's Email Address (if any)

[redacted]

Sponsor's Declaration and Certification

Copies of any documents I have submitted are exact photocopies of unaltered, original documents, and I understand that USCIS or the U.S. Department of State (DOS) may require that I submit original documents to USCIS or DOS at a later date. Furthermore, I authorize the release of any information from any and all of my records that USCIS or DOS may need to determine my eligibility for the benefit that I seek.

I furthermore authorize release of information contained in this affidavit, in supporting documents, and in my USCIS or DOS records, to other entities and persons where necessary for the administration and enforcement of U.S. immigration law.

I certify, under penalty of perjury, that all of the information in my affidavit and any document submitted with it were provided or authorized by me, that I reviewed and understand all of the information contained in, and submitted with, my affidavit and that all of this information is complete, true, and correct.

A. I know the contents of this affidavit of support that I signed;

B. I have read and I understand each of the obligations described in Part 8., and I agree, freely and without any mental reservation or purpose of evasion, to accept each of those obligations in order to make it possible for the immigrants indicated in Part 3. to become lawful permanent residents of the United States;

C. I agree to submit to the personal jurisdiction of any Federal or state court that has subject matter jurisdiction of a lawsuit against me to enforce my obligations under this Form I-864;

Part 8. Sponsor's Contract, Statement, Contact Information, Declaration, Certification, and Signature (continued)

D. Each of the Federal income tax returns submitted in support of this affidavit are true copies, or are unaltered tax transcripts, of the tax returns I filed with the IRS;

E. I understand that, if I am related to the sponsored immigrant by marriage, the termination of the marriage (by divorce, dissolution, annulment, or other legal process) will not relieve me of my obligations under this Form I-864; and

F. I authorize the Social Security Administration to release information about me in its records to USCIS and DOS.

Sponsor's Signature

6.a. [redacted]

6.b. Date of Signature (mm/dd/yyyy) 7/19/18

NOTE TO ALL SPONSORS: If you do not completely fill out this affidavit or fail to submit required documents listed in the Instructions, USCIS or DOS may deny your affidavit.

Part 9. Interpreter's Contact Information, Certification, and Signature

Provide the following information about the interpreter.

Interpreter's Full Name

1.a. Interpreter's Family Name (Last Name)

1.b. Interpreter's Given Name (First Name)

2. Interpreter's Business or Organization Name (if any)

Interpreter's Mailing Address

3.a. Street Number and Name

3.b. ☐ Apt. ☐ Ste. ☐ Flr.

3.c. City or Town

3.d. State 3.e. ZIP Code

3.f. Province

3.g. Postal Code

3.h. Country

Interpreter's Contact Information

4. Interpreter's Daytime Telephone Number

5. Interpreter's Mobile Telephone Number (if any)

6. Interpreter's Email Address (if any)

Interpreter's Certification

I certify, under penalty of perjury, that:

I am fluent in English and ______, which is the same language specified in Part 8., Item Number 1.b., and I have read to this sponsor in the identified language every question and instruction on this affidavit and his or her answer to every question. The sponsor informed me that he or she understands every instruction, question, and answer on the affidavit, including the **Sponsor's Declaration and Certification**, and has verified the accuracy of every answer.

Interpreter's Signature

7.a. Interpreter's Signature

7.b. Date of Signature (mm/dd/yyyy)

Part 10. Contact Information, Declaration, and Signature of the Person Preparing this Affidavit, if Other Than the Sponsor

Provide the following information about the preparer.

Preparer's Full Name

1.a. Preparer's Family Name (Last Name)
Reed

1.b. Preparer's Given Name (First Name)
Christopher

2. Preparer's Business or Organization Name (if any)
Law Offices of Brian D. Lerner, APC

Preparer's Mailing Address

3.a. Street Number and Name: 3233 E. Broadway

3.b. ☐ Apt. ☐ Ste. ☐ Flr.

3.c. City or Town: Long Beach

3.d. State: CA 3.e. ZIP Code: 90803

3.f. Province

3.g. Postal Code

3.h. Country
USA

Preparer's Contact Information

4. Preparer's Daytime Telephone Number
(562) 495-0554

5. Preparer's Mobile Telephone Number (if any)

6. Preparer's Email Address (if any)
creed@eimmigration.org

Preparer's Statement

7.a. ☐ I am not an attorney or accredited representative but have prepared this affidavit on behalf of the sponsor and with the sponsor's consent.

7.b. ☒ I am an attorney or accredited representative and my representation of the sponsor in this case ☒ extends ☐ does not extend beyond the preparation of this affidavit.

NOTE: If you are an attorney or accredited representative, you may be obliged to submit a completed Form G-28, Notice of Entry of Appearance as Attorney or Accredited Representative, or G-28I, Notice of Entry of Appearance as Attorney In Matters Outside the Geographical Confines of the United States, with this affidavit.

Preparer's Certification

By my signature, I certify, under penalty of perjury, that I prepared this affidavit at the request of the sponsor. The sponsor then reviewed this completed affidavit and informed me that he or she understands all of the information contained in, and submitted with, his or her affidavit, including the Sponsor's Declaration and Certification, and that all of this information is complete, true, and correct. I completed this affidavit based only on information that the sponsor provided to me or authorized me to obtain or use.

Preparer's Signature

8.a. Preparer's Signature

8.b. Date of Signature (mm/dd/yyyy) 7/23/15

Part 11. Additional Information

If you need extra space to provide any additional information within this affidavit, use the space below. If you need more space than what is provided, you may make copies of this page to complete and file with this affidavit or attach a separate sheet of paper. Type or print your name and A-Number (if any) at the top of each sheet; indicate the **Page Number**, **Part Number**, and **Item Number** to which your answer refers; and sign and date each sheet.

1.a. Family Name (Last Name) [redacted]

1.b. Given Name (First Name) [redacted]

1.c. Middle Name [redacted]

2. A-Number (if any) ► A-

3.a. Page Number 5 3.b. Part Number 6 3.c. Item Number 24a

3.d. Total income from the Petitioner was not from employment but from Lottery winnings.

4.a. Page Number 4.b. Part Number 4.c. Item Number

4.d.

5.a. Page Number 5.b. Part Number 5.c. Item Number

5.d.

6.a. Page Number 6.b. Part Number 6.c. Item Number

6.d.

7.a. Page Number 7.b. Part Number 7.c. Item Number

7.d.

Affidavit of Support Under Section 213A of the INA

Department of Homeland Security
U.S. Citizenship and Immigration Services

USCIS
Form I-864
OMB No. 1615-0075
Expires 03/31/2020

For USCIS Use Only	Affidavit of Support Submitter	Section 213A Review	Number of Support Affidavits in File
	☐ Petitioner ☐ 1st Joint Sponsor ☐ 2nd Joint Sponsor ☐ Substitute Sponsor ☐ 5% Owner	☐ MEETS requirements ☐ DOES NOT MEET requirements Reviewed By ________ Office ________ Date (mm/dd/yyyy) ________	☐ 1 ☐ 2 Remarks

To be completed by an attorney or accredited representative (if any).	☒ Select this box if Form G-28 or G-28I is attached.	Attorney State Bar Number (if applicable)	Attorney or Accredited Representative USCIS Online Account Number (if any)
		235438	

► START HERE - Type or print in black ink.

Part 1. Basis For Filing Affidavit of Support

1. I, Charina [redacted] JOHNSON
am the sp[redacted]mitting this affidavit of support because (Select only one box):

1.a. ☐ I am the petitioner. I filed or am filing for the immigration of my relative.

1.b. ☐ I filed an alien worker petition on behalf of the intending immigrant, who is related to me as my

1.c. ☐ I have an ownership interest of at least 5 percent in

which filed an alien worker petition on behalf of the intending immigrant, who is related to me as my

1.d. ☒ I am the only joint sponsor.

1.e. ☐ I am the ☐ first ☐ second of two joint sponsors.

1.f. ☐ The original petitioner is deceased. I am the substitute sponsor. I am the intending immigrant's

NOTE: If you are filing this form as a sponsor, you must include proof of your U.S. citizenship, U.S. national status, or lawful permanent resident status.

Mailing Address

2.a. In Care Of Name

2.b. Street Number and Name [redacted]

2.c. ☐ Apt. ☐ Ste. ☐ Flr. 5C

2.d. City or Town [redacted]

2.e. State CA 2.f. ZIP Code [redacted]

2.g. Province

2.h. Postal Code

2.i. Country
USA

Other Information

3. Country of Citizenship or Nationality
Philippines

4. Date of Birth (mm/dd/yyyy) 01/04/1980

5. Alien Registration Number (A-Number) (if any)
► A-

6. USCIS Online Account Number (if any)
►

7. Daytime Telephone Number
[redacted]

Part 2. Information About the Principal Immigrant

1.a. Family Name (Last Name) [redacted]

1.b. Given Name (First Name) [redacted]

Part 3. Information About the Immigrants You Are Sponsoring

1. I am sponsoring the principal immigrant named in Part 2.

[X] Yes [ ] No (Applicable only if you are sponsoring family members in Part 3. as the second joint sponsor or if you are sponsoring family members who are immigrating more than six months after the principal immigrant)

2. [ ] I am sponsoring the following family members immigrating at the same time or within six months of the principal immigrant named in Part 2. (Do not include any relative listed on a separate visa petition.)

3. [ ] I am sponsoring the following family members who are immigrating more than six months after the principal immigrant.

Family Member 1

4.a. Family Name (Last Name)

4.b. Given Name (First Name)

4.c. Middle Name

5. Relationship to Principal Immigrant

6. Date of Birth (mm/dd/yyyy)

7. Alien Registration Number (A-Number) (if any) ▶ A-

8. USCIS Online Account Number (if any) ▶

Family Member 2

9.a. Family Name (Last Name)

9.b. Given Name (First Name)

9.c. Middle Name

10. Relationship to Principal Immigrant

11. Date of Birth (mm/dd/yyyy)

12. Alien Registration Number (A-Number) (if any) ▶ A-

13. USCIS Online Account Number (if any) ▶

Family Member 3

14.a. Family Name (Last Name)

14.b. Given Name (First Name)

14.c. Middle Name

15. Relationship to Principal Immigrant

16. Date of Birth (mm/dd/yyyy)

17. Alien Registration Number (A-Number) (if any) ▶ A-

18. USCIS Online Account Number (if any) ▶

Family Member 4

19.a. Family Name (Last Name)

19.b. Given Name (First Name)

19.c. Middle Name

20. Relationship to Principal Immigrant

21. Date of Birth (mm/dd/yyyy)

22. Alien Registration Number (A-Number) (if any) ▶ A-

23. USCIS Online Account Number (if any) ▶

Family Member 5

24.a. Family Name (Last Name)

24.b. Given Name (First Name)

24.c. Middle Name

25. Relationship to Principal Immigrant

26. Date of Birth (mm/dd/yyyy)

27. Alien Registration Number (A-Number) (if any) ▶ A-

28. USCIS Online Account Number (if any) ▶

Part 3. Information About the Immigrants You Are Sponsoring (continued)

29. Enter the total number of immigrants you are sponsoring on this affidavit which includes the principal immigrant listed in Part 2., any immigrants listed in Part 3., Item Numbers 1 - 28. and (if applicable), any immigrants listed for these questions in Part 11. Additional Information. Do not count the principal immigrant if you are only sponsoring family members entering more than 6 months after the principal immigrant.

1

Part 4. Information About You (Sponsor)

Sponsor's Full Name

1.a. Family Name (Last Name) JOHNSON [redacted]

1.b. Given Name (First Name) Charina

1.c. Middle Name [redacted]

Sponsor's Mailing Address

2.a. In Care Of Name

2.b. Street Number and Name [redacted]

2.c. ☐ Apt. ☐ Ste. ☐ Flr.

2.d. City or Town [redacted]

2.e. State CA 2.f. ZIP Code [redacted]

2.g. Province

2.h. Postal Code

2.i. Country USA

3. Is your current mailing address the same as your physical address? ☒ Yes ☐ No

If you answered "No" to Item Number 3., provide your physical address in Item Numbers 4.a. - 4.h.

Sponsor's Physical Address

4.a. Street Number and Name

4.b. ☐ Apt. ☐ Ste. ☐ Flr.

4.c. City or Town

4.d. State 4.e. ZIP Code

4.f. Province

4.g. Postal Code

4.h. Country

Other Information

5. Country of Domicile

6. Date of Birth (mm/dd/yyyy) 04/05/1967

7. City or Town of Birth Binghamton

8. State or Province of Birth New York

9. Country of Birth USA

10. U.S. Social Security Number (Required) ► [redacted]

Citizenship or Residency

11.a. ☒ I am a U.S. citizen.

11.b. ☐ I am a U.S. national.

11.c. ☐ I am a lawful permanent resident.

12. Sponsor's A-Number (if any) ► A-

13. Sponsor's USCIS Online Account Number (if any) ►

Military Service (To be completed by petitioner sponsors only.)

14. I am currently on active duty in the U.S. Armed Forces or U.S. Coast Guard. ☐ Yes ☒ No

For USCIS Use Only

Part 5. Sponsor's Household Size

NOTE: Do not count any member of your household more than once.

Persons you are sponsoring in this affidavit:

1. Provide the number you entered in Part 3., Item Number 29. 1

Persons NOT sponsored in this affidavit:

2. Yourself. 1
3. If you are currently married, enter "1" for your spouse.
4. If you have dependent children, enter the number here.
5. If you have any other dependents, enter the number here.
6. If you have sponsored any other persons on Form I-864 or Form I-864EZ who are now lawful permanent residents, enter the number here.
7. **OPTIONAL:** If you have siblings, parents, or adult children with the same principal residence who are combining their income with yours by submitting Form I-864A, enter the number here.
8. Add together Part 5., Item Numbers 1. - 7. and enter the number here. Household Size: 2

Part 6. Sponsor's Employment and Income

I am currently:

1. [X] Employed as a/an Nurse
2. Name of Employer 1 AHMC San Gabriel Valley Medical Center LP
3. Name of Employer 2 (if applicable)
4. [ ] Self-Employed as a/an (Occupation)
5. [ ] Retired Since (mm/dd/yyyy)
6. [ ] Unemployed Since (mm/dd/yyyy)
7. My current individual annual income is: $ 106998

Income you are using from any other person who was counted in your household size, including, in certain conditions, the intending immigrant. (See Form I-864 Instructions.) Please indicate name, relationship, and income.

Person 1

8. Name
9. Relationship
10. Current Income $ 0

Person 2

11. Name
12. Relationship
13. Current Income $ 0

Person 3

14. Name
15. Relationship
16. Current Income $ 0

Person 4

17. Name
18. Relationship

For USCIS Use Only	Household Size	Poverty Guideline	Remarks
	☐ 1 ☐ 2 ☐ 3 ☐ 4 ☐ 5 ☐ 6 ☐ 7 ☐ 8 ☐ 9 ☐ Other: ____	Year: 20____ Poverty Line $ ____	

Part 6. Sponsor's Employment and Income (continued)

20. **My Current Annual Household Income** (Total all lines from **Part 6.**, **Item Numbers 7.**, **10.**, **13.**, **16.**, and **19.**; the total will be compared to Federal Poverty Guidelines on Form I-864P.) $ 106998

21. ☒ The people listed in **Item Numbers 8.**, **11.**, **14.**, and **17.** have completed Form I-864A. I am filing along with this affidavit all necessary Form I-864As completed by these people.

22. ☐ One or more of the people listed in **Item Numbers 8.**, **11.**, **14.**, and **17.** do not need to complete Form I-864A because he or she is the intending immigrant and has no accompanying dependents.

Name ____

Federal Income Tax Return Information

23.a. Have you filed a Federal income tax return for each of the three most recent tax years? ☒ Yes ☐ No

NOTE: You **MUST** attach a photocopy or transcript of your Federal income tax return for only the most recent tax year.

23.b. ☐ (Optional) I have attached photocopies or transcripts of my Federal income tax returns for my second and third most recent tax years.

My total income (adjusted gross income on Internal Revenue Service (IRS) Form 1040EZ) as reported on my Federal income tax returns for the most recent three years was:

	Tax Year	Total Income
24.a. Most Recent	2017	$ 156,822.00
24.b. 2nd Most Recent	2016	$ 163,565.00
24.c. 3rd Most Recent	2015	$ 153,701.00

25. ☐ I was not required to file a Federal income tax return as my income was below the IRS required level and I have attached evidence to support this.

Part 7. Use of Assets to Supplement Income (Optional)

If your income, or the total income for you and your household, from **Part 6.**, **Item Numbers 20.** or **24.a.** - **24.c.**, exceeds the Federal Poverty Guidelines for your household size, **YOU ARE NOT REQUIRED** to complete this **Part 7.** Skip to **Part 8.**

Your Assets (Optional)

1. Enter the balance of all savings and checking accounts. $ ____

2. Enter the net cash value of real-estate holdings. (Net value means current assessed value minus mortgage debt.) $ ____

3. Enter the net cash value of all stocks, bonds, certificates of deposit, and any other assets not already included in **Item Number 1.** or **Item Number 2.** $ ____

4. Add together **Item Numbers 1.** - **3.** and enter the number here. **TOTAL:** $ ____

Assets from Form I-864A, Part 4., Item Number 3.d., for:

5.a. Name of Relative ____

5.b. Your household member's assets from Form I-864A (optional). $ ____

Assets of the principal sponsored immigrant (optional)

The principal sponsored immigrant is the person listed in **Part 2.**, **Item Numbers 1.a.** - **1.c.** Only include the assets if the principal immigrant is being sponsored by this affidavit of support.

6. Enter the balance of the principal immigrant's savings and checking accounts. $ ____

7. Enter the net cash value of all the principal immigrant's real estate holdings. (Net value means investment value minus mortgage debt.) $ ____

8. Enter the current cash value of the principal immigrant's stocks, bonds, certificates of deposit, and other assets not included in **Item Number 6.** or **Item Number 7.** $ ____

For USCIS Use Only	Household Size	Poverty Guideline	Sponsor's Household Income (Page 5, Line 10)	Remarks
	☐ 1 ☐ 2 ☐ 3 ☐ 4 ☐ 5 ☐ 6	Year: 20___	$	
	☐ 7 ☐ 8 ☐ 9 ☐ Other_____	Poverty Line $	*The total value of all assets, line 10, must equal 5 times (3 times for spouses and children of USCs, or 1 time for orphans to be formally adopted in the U.S.) the difference between the poverty guidelines and the sponsor's household income, line 10.*	

Part 7. Use of Assets to Supplement Income (Optional) (continued)

9. Add together Item Numbers 6. - 8. and enter the number here. $

Total Value of Assets

10. Add together Item Numbers 4., 5.b., and 9. and enter the number here.

TOTAL: $

Part 8. Sponsor's Contract, Statement, Contact Information, Declaration, Certification, and Signature

NOTE: Read the Penalties section of the Form I-864 Instructions before completing this part.

Sponsor's Contract

Please note that, by signing this Form I-864, you agree to assume certain specific obligations under the Immigration and Nationality Act (INA) and other Federal laws. The following paragraphs describe those obligations. Please read the following information carefully before you sign Form I-864. If you do not understand the obligations, you may wish to consult an attorney or accredited representative.

What is the Legal Effect of My Signing Form I-864?

If you sign Form I-864 on behalf of any person (called the intending immigrant) who is applying for an immigrant visa or for adjustment of status to a lawful permanent resident, and that intending immigrant submits Form I-864 to the U.S. Government with his or her application for an immigrant visa or adjustment of status, under INA section 213A, these actions create a contract between you and the U.S. Government. The intending immigrant becoming a lawful permanent resident is the consideration for the contract.

Under this contract, you agree that, in deciding whether the intending immigrant can establish that he or she is not inadmissible to the United States as a person likely to become a public charge, the U.S. Government can consider your income and assets as available for the support of the intending immigrant.

What If I Choose Not to Sign Form I-864?

The U.S. Government cannot make you sign Form I-864 if you do not want to do so. But if you do not sign Form I-864, the intending immigrant may not become a lawful permanent resident in the United States.

What Does Signing Form I-864 Require Me To Do?

If an intending immigrant becomes a lawful permanent resident in the United States based on a Form I-864 that you have signed, then, until your obligations under Form I-864 terminate, you must:

A. Provide the intending immigrant any support necessary to maintain him or her at an income that is at least 125 percent of the Federal Poverty Guidelines for his or her household size (100 percent if you are the petitioning sponsor and are on active duty in the U.S. Armed Forces or U.S. Coast Guard, and the person is your husband, wife, or unmarried child under 21 years of age); and

B. Notify U.S. Citizenship and Immigration Services (USCIS) of any change in your address, within 30 days of the change, by filing Form I-865.

What Other Consequences Are There?

If an intending immigrant becomes a lawful permanent resident in the United States based on a Form I-864 that you have signed, then, until your obligations under Form I-864 terminate, the U.S. Government may consider (deem) your income and assets as available to that person, in determining whether he or she is eligible for certain Federal means-tested public benefits and also for state or local means-tested public benefits, if the state or local government's rules provide for consideration (deeming) of your income and assets as available to the person.

This provision does not apply to public benefits specified in section 403(c) of the Welfare Reform Act such as emergency Medicaid, short-term, non-cash emergency relief; services provided under the National School Lunch and Child Nutrition Acts; immunizations and testing and treatment for communicable diseases; and means-tested programs under the Elementary and Secondary Education Act.

What If I Do Not Fulfill My Obligations?

If you do not provide sufficient support to the person who becomes a lawful permanent resident based on a Form I-864 that you signed, that person may sue you for this support.

Part 8. Sponsor's Contract, Statement, Contact Information, Declaration, Certification, and Signature (continued)

If a Federal, state, local, or private agency provided any covered means-tested public benefit to the person who becomes a lawful permanent resident based on a Form I-864 that you signed, the agency may ask you to reimburse them for the amount of the benefits they provided. If you do not make the reimbursement, the agency may sue you for the amount that the agency believes you owe.

If you are sued, and the court enters a judgment against you, the person or agency that sued you may use any legally permitted procedures for enforcing or collecting the judgment. You may also be required to pay the costs of collection, including attorney fees.

If you do not file a properly completed Form I-865 within 30 days of any change of address, USCIS may impose a civil fine for your failing to do so.

When Will These Obligations End?

Your obligations under a Form I-864 that you signed will end if the person who becomes a lawful permanent resident based on that affidavit:

A. Becomes a U.S. citizen;

B. Has worked, or can receive credit for, 40 quarters of coverage under the Social Security Act;

C. No longer has lawful permanent resident status and has departed the United States;

D. Is subject to removal, but applies for and obtains, in removal proceedings, a new grant of adjustment of status, based on a new affidavit of support, if one is required; or

E. Dies.

NOTE: Divorce does not terminate your obligations under Form I-864.

Your obligations under a Form I-864 that you signed also end if you die. Therefore, if you die, your estate is not required to take responsibility for the person's support after your death. However, your estate may owe any support that you accumulated before you died.

Sponsor's Statement

NOTE: Select the box for either Item Number 1.a. or 1.b. If applicable, select the box for Item Number 2.

1.a. [X] I can read and understand English, and I have read and understand every question and instruction on this affidavit and my answer to every question.

1.b. [ ] The interpreter named in Part 9. read to me every question and instruction on this affidavit and my answer to every question in

a language in which I am fluent, and I understood everything.

2. [X] At my request, the preparer named in Part 10.,

Christopher A Reed

prepared this affidavit for me based only upon information I provided or authorized.

Sponsor's Contact Information

3. Sponsor's Daytime Telephone Number

[redacted]

4. Sponsor's Mobile Telephone Number (if any)

5. Sponsor's Email Address (if any)

[redacted]

Sponsor's Declaration and Certification

Copies of any documents I have submitted are exact photocopies of unaltered, original documents, and I understand that USCIS or the U.S. Department of State (DOS) may require that I submit original documents to USCIS or DOS at a later date. Furthermore, I authorize the release of any information from any and all of my records that USCIS or DOS may need to determine my eligibility for the benefit that I seek.

I furthermore authorize release of information contained in this affidavit, in supporting documents, and in my USCIS or DOS records, to other entities and persons where necessary for the administration and enforcement of U.S. immigration law.

I certify, under penalty of perjury, that all of the information in my affidavit and any document submitted with it were provided or authorized by me, that I reviewed and understand all of the information contained in, and submitted with, my affidavit and that all of this information is complete, true, and correct.

A. I know the contents of this affidavit of support that I signed;

B. I have read and I understand each of the obligations described in Part 8., and I agree, freely and without any mental reservation or purpose of evasion, to accept each of those obligations in order to make it possible for the immigrants indicated in Part 3. to become lawful permanent residents of the United States;

C. I agree to submit to the personal jurisdiction of any Federal or state court that has subject matter

Part 8. Sponsor's Contract, Statement, Contact Information, Declaration, Certification, and Signature (continued)

D. Each of the Federal income tax returns submitted in support of this affidavit are true copies, or are unaltered tax transcripts, of the tax returns I filed with the IRS;

E. I understand that, if I am related to the sponsored immigrant by marriage, the termination of the marriage (by divorce, dissolution, annulment, or other legal process) will not relieve me of my obligations under this Form I-864; and

F. I authorize the Social Security Administration to release information about me in its records to USCIS and DOS.

Sponsor's Signature

6.a. Sponsor's Signature [redacted]

6.b. Date of Signature (mm/dd/yyyy) 01-19-2018

NOTE TO ALL SPONSORS: If you do not completely fill out this affidavit or fail to submit required documents listed in the Instructions, USCIS or DOS may deny your affidavit.

Part 9. Interpreter's Contact Information, Certification, and Signature

Provide the following information about the interpreter.

Interpreter's Full Name

1.a. Interpreter's Family Name (Last Name)

1.b. Interpreter's Given Name (First Name)

2. Interpreter's Business or Organization Name (if any)

Interpreter's Mailing Address

3.a. Street Number and Name

3.b. ☐ Apt. ☐ Ste. ☐ Flr.

3.c. City or Town

3.d. State 3.e. ZIP Code

3.f. Province

3.g. Postal Code

3.h. Country

Interpreter's Contact Information

4. Interpreter's Daytime Telephone Number

5. Interpreter's Mobile Telephone Number (if any)

6. Interpreter's Email Address (if any)

Interpreter's Certification

I certify, under penalty of perjury, that:

I am fluent in English and ______,

which is the same language specified in **Part 8., Item Number 1.b.**, and I have read to this sponsor in the identified language every question and instruction on this affidavit and his or her answer to every question. The sponsor informed me that he or she understands every instruction, question, and answer on the affidavit, including the **Sponsor's Declaration and Certification**, and has verified the accuracy of every answer.

Interpreter's Signature

7.a. Interpreter's Signature

7.b. Date of Signature (mm/dd/yyyy)

Part 10. Contact Information, Declaration, and Signature of the Person Preparing this Affidavit, if Other Than the Sponsor

Provide the following information about the preparer:

Preparer's Full Name

1.a. Preparer's Family Name (Last Name)
Reed

1.b. Preparer's Given Name (First Name)
Christopher

2. Preparer's Business or Organization Name (if any)
Law Offices of Brian D. Lerner, APC

Preparer's Mailing Address

3.a. Street Number and Name: 3233 E. Broadway

3.b. ☐ Apt. ☐ Ste. ☐ Flr.

3.c. City or Town: Long Beach

3.d. State: CA 3.e. ZIP Code: 90803

3.f. Province

3.g. Postal Code

3.h. Country
USA

Preparer's Contact Information

4. Preparer's Daytime Telephone Number
(562) 495-0554

5. Preparer's Mobile Telephone Number (if any)

6. Preparer's Email Address (if any)
creed@eimmigration.org

Preparer's Statement

7.a. ☐ I am not an attorney or accredited representative but have prepared this affidavit on behalf of the sponsor and with the sponsor's consent.

7.b. ☒ I am an attorney or accredited representative and my representation of the sponsor in this case ☒ extends ☐ does not extend beyond the preparation of this affidavit.

NOTE: If you are an attorney or accredited representative, you may be obliged to submit a completed Form G-28, Notice of Entry of Appearance as Attorney or Accredited Representative, or G-28I, Notice of Entry of Appearance as Attorney In Matters Outside the Geographical Confines of the United States, with this affidavit.

Preparer's Certification

By my signature, I certify, under penalty of perjury, that I prepared this affidavit at the request of the sponsor. The sponsor then reviewed this completed affidavit and informed me that he or she understands all of the information contained in, and submitted with, his or her affidavit, including the Sponsor's Declaration and Certification, and that all of this information is complete, true, and correct. I completed this affidavit based only on information that the sponsor provided to me or authorized me to obtain or use.

Preparer's Signature

8.a. Preparer's Signature

8.b. Date of Signature (mm/dd/yyyy) 7/02/18

Part 11. Additional Information

If you need extra space to provide any additional information within this affidavit, use the space below. If you need more space than what is provided, you may make copies of this page to complete and file with this affidavit or attach a separate sheet of paper. Type or print your name and A-Number (if any) at the top of each sheet; indicate the **Page Number**, **Part Number**, and **Item Number** to which your answer refers; and sign and date each sheet.

1.a. Family Name (Last Name) [redacted]

1.b. Given Name (First Name) Charina

1.c. Middle Name [redacted]

2. A-Number (if any) ► A-

3.a. Page Number 3.b. Part Number 3.c. Item Number

3.d.

4.a. Page Number 4.b. Part Number 4.c. Item Number

4.d.

5.a. Page Number 5.b. Part Number 5.c. Item Number

5.d.

6.a. Page Number 6.b. Part Number 6.c. Item Number

6.d.

7.a. Page Number 7.b. Part Number 7.c. Item Number

7.d.

SECTION 3:
EXHIBITS

Exhibit '1'

Copy of the Birth Certificate of the Petitioner

CERTIFIED TRANSCRIPT OF BIRTH

STATE OF NEW YORK

DEPARTMENT OF HEALTH

Full Name of Child: [redacted] Glenn [redacted]

Sex: Male

Date of Birth: 04/05/1967 07:12 AM

Place of Birth: Binghamton, New York

Name of Mother: Eleanor Louise Finn

Name of Father: Warwick Adelbert [redacted]

Date Filed: 04/13/1967

State File Number: 039642

This is to certify that the information concerning the birth of the above named person is a true and accurate transcription of the information recorded on the original certificate of birth on file with the New York State Department of Health.

Robert LoCicero
Director of Vital Records

Date: 01/24/2017

Do not accept this transcript unless the raised seal of the New York State Department of Health is affixed thereon.

NOTE CAREFULLY: Any alteration voids this transcript

A17024008 | V995631500

Exhibit '2'

Copy of the Marriage Certificate of the Petitioner and the Beneficiary

Inst #: 200912140002837
Fees: $10.00
12/14/2009 03:17:00 PM
Receipt #: 160740
Requestor:
RECORDER CLARK COUNTY
Recorded By: DBX Pgs: 1
DEBBIE CONWAY
CLARK COUNTY RECORDER

STATE OF NEVADA
MARRIAGE CERTIFICATE
No. 20091 21 280003450

STATE OF NEVADA }
COUNTY OF CLARK } ss

This is to certify that the undersigned, BIANCA MORRIS DEPUTY MARRIAGE COMMISSIONER
(print name and title of official performing marriage)

did on the 12th day of the month of DECEMBER of the year 20 09,

at 309 SOUTH THIRD STREET (address or church) LAS VEGAS (city), Nevada,

join in lawful wedlock [redacted] (groom)

of MONROE (city), State/Country of NORTH CAROLINA

date of birth [illegible]

and [redacted]

of LOS ANGELES (city), State/Country of CALIFORNIA

date of birth [illegible]

with their mutual consent, in the presence of TONIROSE PALACIOS (witness)

SEAL

Signature of Official Performing Marriage (Black Ink Only)

BIANCA MORRIS
DEPUTY COMMISSIONER OF CIVIL MARRIAGES
Print Name and Title of Official

309 SOUTH THIRD STREET
Address of Official Performing Marriage

LAS VEGAS, NEVADA 89101
City, State and Zip Code

DIANA ALBA, COUNTY CLERK

Bride/Groom Mailing Address: 1325 HUNTINGTON DR NORTH # 183
LOS ANGELES, CA 90032

This Certificate must be typewritten or printed in black ink and presented within 10 days to the Clark County Recorder, 500 S. Grand Central Parkway, Las Vegas, Nevada 89155-1510

Exhibit '3'

Copy of the Joint 2017 Tax Return of the Petitioner and the Beneficiary

Form **1040** Department of the Treasury—Internal Revenue Service (99)
U.S. Individual Income Tax Return **2017** OMB No. 1545-0074 IRS Use Only—Do not write or staple in this space.

For the year Jan. 1–Dec. 31, 2017, or other tax year beginning , 2017, ending , 20 | See separate instructions.

Your first name and initial: [redacted] | Last name: [redacted] | Your social security number: [redacted]

If a joint return, spouse's first name and initial: [redacted] | Last name: [redacted] | Spouse's social security number: [redacted]

Home address (number and street). If you have a P.O. box, see instructions. [redacted] | Apt. no. 5C | Make sure the SSN(s) above and on line 6c are correct.

City, town or post office, state, and ZIP code. If you have a foreign address, also complete spaces below (see instructions). [redacted]

Foreign country name | Foreign province/state/county | Foreign postal code

Presidential Election Campaign: Check here if you, or your spouse if filing jointly, want $3 to go to this fund. Checking a box below will not change your tax or refund. [X] You [ ] Spouse

Filing Status — Check only one box.
1 [ ] Single
2 [X] Married filing jointly (even if only one had income)
3 [ ] Married filing separately. Enter spouse's SSN above and full name here. ▶
4 [ ] Head of household (with qualifying person). (See instructions.) If the qualifying person is a child but not your dependent, enter this child's name here. ▶
5 [ ] Qualifying widow(er) (see instructions)

Exemptions
6a [X] Yourself. If someone can claim you as a dependent, do not check box 6a
b [X] Spouse
Boxes checked on 6a and 6b: 2

c Dependents:

(1) First name Last name	(2) Dependent's social security number	(3) Dependent's relationship to you	(4) ✓ if child under age 17 qualifying for child tax credit (see instructions)
			[ ]
			[ ]
			[ ]
			[ ]

If more than four dependents, see instructions and check here ▶ [ ]

No. of children on 6c who: • lived with you; • did not live with you due to divorce or separation (see instructions); Dependents on 6c not entered above

d Total number of exemptions claimed — Add numbers on lines above ▶ 2

Income

Attach Form(s) W-2 here. Also attach Forms W-2G and 1099-R if tax was withheld. If you did not get a W-2, see instructions.

7	Wages, salaries, tips, etc. Attach Form(s) W-2		
8a	Taxable interest. Attach Schedule B if required		
b	Tax-exempt interest. Do not include on line 8a	8b	
9a	Ordinary dividends. Attach Schedule B if required		
b	Qualified dividends	9b	
10	Taxable refunds, credits, or offsets of state and local income taxes		
11	Alimony received		
12	Business income or (loss). Attach Schedule C or C-EZ		1,165.
13	Capital gain or (loss). Attach Schedule D if required. If not required, check here ▶ [ ]		
14	Other gains or (losses). Attach Form 4797		
15a	IRA distributions	15a	b Taxable amount 15b
16a	Pensions and annuities	16a	b Taxable amount 16b
17	Rental real estate, royalties, partnerships, S corporations, trusts, etc. Attach Schedule E		
18	Farm income or (loss). Attach Schedule F		
19	Unemployment compensation		
20a	Social security benefits	20a	b Taxable amount 20b
21	Other income. List type and amount Gambling Winnings		1,521.
22	Combine the amounts in the far right column for lines 7 through 21. This is your total income ▶		2,686.

Adjusted Gross Income

23	Educator expenses	
24	Certain business expenses of reservists, performing artists, and fee-basis government officials. Attach Form 2106 or 2106-EZ	
25	Health savings account deduction. Attach Form 8889	
26	Moving expenses. Attach Form 3903	
27	Deductible part of self-employment tax. Attach Schedule SE	83.
28	Self-employed SEP, SIMPLE, and qualified plans	
29	Self-employed health insurance deduction	
30	Penalty on early withdrawal of savings	
31a	Alimony paid b Recipient's SSN ▶	
32	IRA deduction	
33	Student loan interest deduction	
34	Reserved for future use	

Form 1040 (2017) Page 2

Tax and Credits	38	Amount from line 37 (adjusted gross income)		38	2,603.
	39a	Check if: ☐ You were born before January 2, 1953, ☐ Blind. ☐ Spouse was born before January 2, 1953, ☐ Blind. Total boxes checked ▶ 39a ☐			
	b	If your spouse itemizes on a separate return or you were a dual-status alien, check here ▶ 39b ☐			
Standard Deduction for— • People who check any box on line 39a or 39b or who can be claimed as a dependent, see instructions. • All others: Single or Married filing separately, $6,350 Married filing jointly or Qualifying widow(er), $12,700 Head of household, $9,350	40	Itemized deductions (from Schedule A) or your standard deduction (see left margin)		40	12,700.
	41	Subtract line 40 from line 38		41	-10,097.
	42	Exemptions. If line 38 is $156,900 or less, multiply $4,050 by the number on line 6d. Otherwise, see instructions		42	8,100.
	43	Taxable income. Subtract line 42 from line 41. If line 42 is more than line 41, enter -0-		43	0.
	44	Tax (see instructions). Check if any from: a ☐ Form(s) 8814 b ☐ Form 4972 c ☐		44	0.
	45	Alternative minimum tax (see instructions). Attach Form 6251		45	
	46	Excess advance premium tax credit repayment. Attach Form 8962		46	
	47	Add lines 44, 45, and 46 ▶		47	0.
	48	Foreign tax credit. Attach Form 1116 if required	48		
	49	Credit for child and dependent care expenses. Attach Form 2441	49		
	50	Education credits from Form 8863, line 19	50		
	51	Retirement savings contributions credit. Attach Form 8880	51		
	52	Child tax credit. Attach Schedule 8812, if required	52		
	53	Residential energy credit. Attach Form 5695	53		
	54	Other credits from Form: a ☐ 3800 b ☐ 8801 c ☐	54		
	55	Add lines 48 through 54. These are your total credits		55	
	56	Subtract line 55 from line 47. If line 55 is more than line 47, enter -0- ▶		56	0.
Other Taxes	57	Self-employment tax. Attach Schedule SE		57	165.
	58	Unreported social security and Medicare tax from Form: a ☐ 4137 b ☐ 8919		58	
	59	Additional tax on IRAs, other qualified retirement plans, etc. Attach Form 5329 if required		59	
	60a	Household employment taxes from Schedule H		60a	
	b	First-time homebuyer credit repayment. Attach Form 5405 if required		60b	
	61	Health care: individual responsibility (see instructions) Full-year coverage ☒		61	
	62	Taxes from: a ☐ Form 8959 b ☐ Form 8960 c ☐ Instructions; enter code(s)		62	
	63	Add lines 56 through 62. This is your total tax ▶		63	165.
Payments	64	Federal income tax withheld from Forms W-2 and 1099	64		
If you have a qualifying child, attach Schedule EIC.	65	2017 estimated tax payments and amount applied from 2016 return	65		
	66a	Earned income credit (EIC) No	66a		
	b	Nontaxable combat pay election 66b			
	67	Additional child tax credit. Attach Schedule 8812	67		
	68	American opportunity credit from Form 8863, line 8	68		
	69	Net premium tax credit. Attach Form 8962	69		
	70	Amount paid with request for extension to file	70		
	71	Excess social security and tier 1 RRTA tax withheld	71		
	72	Credit for federal tax on fuels. Attach Form 4136	72		
	73	Credits from Form: a ☐ 2439 b ☐ Reserved c ☐ 8885 d ☐	73		
	74	Add lines 64, 65, 66a, and 67 through 73. These are your total payments ▶			
Refund	75	If line 74 is more than line 63, subtract line 63 from line 74. This is the amount you overpaid		75	
	76a	Amount of line 75 you want refunded to you. If Form 8888 is attached, check here ▶ ☐		76a	
Direct deposit? See instructions.	▶ b	Routing number X X X X X X X X X ▶ c Type: ☐ Checking ☐ Savings			
	▶ d	Account number X X X X X X X X X X X X X X X X X			
	77	Amount of line 75 you want applied to your 2018 estimated tax ▶	77		
Amount You Owe	78	Amount you owe. Subtract line 74 from line 63. For details on how to pay, see instructions ▶		78	165.
	79	Estimated tax penalty (see instructions)	79		

Third Party Designee — Do you want to allow another person to discuss this return with the IRS (see instructions)? ☒ Yes. Complete below. ☐ No

Designee's name ▶ ROLANDO C. NAVARRO Phone no. ▶ (562)490-3717 Personal identification number (PIN) ▶ 62574

Sign Here — Under penalties of perjury, I declare that I have examined this return and accompanying schedules and statements, and to the best of my knowledge and belief, they are true, correct, and accurately list all amounts and sources of income I received during the tax year. Declaration of preparer (other than taxpayer) is based on all information of which preparer has any knowledge.

Joint return? See instructions. Keep a copy for your records.

Your signature	Date	Your occupation	Daytime phone number
		WOODWORKER	
Spouse's signature. If a joint return, both must sign.	Date	Spouse's occupation	If the IRS sent you an Identity Protection PIN, enter it here (see inst.)
		HOUSEWIFE	

Paid Prep

Print/Type preparer's name	Preparer's signature	Date	Check ☒ if self-employed	PTIN
[illegible]	[illegible]	[illegible]		[illegible]

SCHEDULE C-EZ (Form 1040)
Department of the Treasury Internal Revenue Service (99)

Net Profit From Business
(Sole Proprietorship)
▶ Partnerships, joint ventures, etc., generally must file Form 1065 or 1065-B.
▶ Attach to Form 1040, 1040NR, or 1041. ▶ See instructions on page 2.

OMB No. 1545-0074
2017
Attachment Sequence No. 09A

Name of proprietor: [redacted]
Social security number (SSN): [redacted]

Part I General Information

You May Use Schedule C-EZ Instead of Schedule C Only If You:
- Had business expenses of $5,000 or less,
- Use the cash method of accounting,
- Did not have an inventory at any time during the year,
- Did not have a net loss from your business,
- Had only one business as either a sole proprietor, qualified joint venture, or statutory employee,

And You:
- Had no employees during the year,
- Do not deduct expenses for business use of your home,
- Do not have prior year unallowed passive activity losses from this business, and
- Are not required to file Form 4562, Depreciation and Amortization, for this business. See the instructions for Schedule C, line 13, to find out if you must file.

A Principal business or profession, including product or service
SPECIALTY TRADE CONTRACTOR - WOODWORKER

B Enter business code (see page 2) ▶ 2 3 8 9 9 0

C Business name. If no separate business name, leave blank.

D Enter your EIN (see page 2)

E Business address (including suite or room no.). Address not required if same as on page 1 of your tax return.
[redacted]
City, town or post office, state, and ZIP code
[redacted]

F Did you make any payments in 2017 that would require you to file Form(s) 1099? (see the Instructions for Schedule C) . . . ☐ Yes ☒ No

G If "Yes," did you or will you file required Forms 1099? . . . ☐ Yes ☐ No

Part II Figure Your Net Profit

1	Gross receipts. Caution: If this income was reported to you on Form W-2 and the "Statutory employee" box on that form was checked, see Statutory employees in the instructions for Schedule C, line 1, and check here . . . ▶ ☐	1	1,560.
2	Total expenses (see page 2). If more than $5,000, you must use Schedule C . . .	2	395.
3	Net profit. Subtract line 2 from line 1. If less than zero, you must use Schedule C. Enter on both Form 1040, line 12, and Schedule SE, line 2, or on Form 1040NR, line 13, and Schedule SE, line 2 (see page 2). (Statutory employees do not report this amount on Schedule SE, line 2.) Estates and trusts, enter on Form 1041, line 3 . . .	3	1,165.

Part III Information on Your Vehicle. Complete this part only if you are claiming car or truck expenses on line 2.

4 When did you place your vehicle in service for business purposes? (month, day, year) ▶ ....

5 Of the total number of miles you drove your vehicle during 2017, enter the number of miles you used your vehicle for:

a Business .... b Commuting (see page 2) .... c Other ....

6 Was your vehicle available for personal use during off-duty hours? . . . ☐ Yes ☐ No

7 Do you (or your spouse) have another vehicle available for personal use? . . . ☐ Yes ☐ No

8a Do you have evidence to support your deduction? . . . ☐ Yes ☐ No

b If "Yes," is the evidence written? . . . ☐ Yes ☐ No

SCHEDULE SE (Form 1040) Department of the Treasury Internal Revenue Service (99)	**Self-Employment Tax** ▶ Go to www.irs.gov/ScheduleSE for instructions and the latest information. ▶ Attach to Form 1040 or Form 1040NR.	OMB No. [illegible] **2017** Attachment Sequence No. **17**
Name of person with self-employment income (as shown on Form 1040 or Form 1040NR) [redacted]	Social security number of person with **self-employment** income ▶	[redacted]

Before you begin: To determine if you must file Schedule SE, see the instructions.

May I Use Short Schedule SE or Must I Use Long Schedule SE?

Note: Use this flowchart only if you must file Schedule SE. If unsure, see *Who Must File Schedule SE* in the instructions.

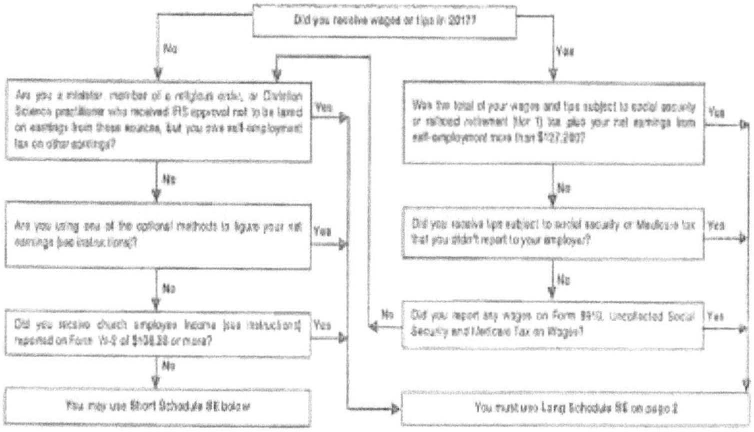

Section A—Short Schedule SE. Caution: Read above to see if you can use Short Schedule SE.

1a	Net farm profit or (loss) from Schedule F, line 34, and farm partnerships, Schedule K-1 (Form 1065), box 14, code A	1a	
b	If you received social security retirement or disability benefits, enter the amount of Conservation Reserve Program payments included on Schedule F, line 4b, or listed on Schedule K-1 (Form 1065), box 20, code Z	1b	( )
2	Net profit or (loss) from Schedule C, line 31; Schedule C-EZ, line 3; Schedule K-1 (Form 1065), box 14, code A (other than farming); and Schedule K-1 (Form 1065-B), box 9, code J1. Ministers and members of religious orders, see instructions for types of income to report on this line. See instructions for other income to report	2	1,165.
3	Combine lines 1a, 1b, and 2	3	1,165.
4	Multiply line 3 by 92.35% (0.9235). If less than $400, you don't owe self-employment tax; don't file this schedule unless you have an amount on line 1b ▶	4	1,076.
	Note: If line 4 is less than $400 due to Conservation Reserve Program payments on line 1b, see instructions.		
5	**Self-employment tax.** If the amount on line 4 is: • $127,200 or less, multiply line 4 by 15.3% (0.153). Enter the result here and on **Form 1040, line 57,** or **Form 1040NR, line 55** • More than $127,200, multiply line 4 by 2.9% (0.029). Then, add $15,772.80 to the result. Enter the total here and on **Form 1040, line 57,** or **Form 1040NR, line 55**	5	165.
6	**Deduction for one-half of self-employment tax.** Multiply line 5 by 50% (0.50). Enter the result here and on **Form 1040, line 27,** or **Form 1040NR, line 27** — 6 — 83.		

For Paperwork Reduction Act Notice, see your tax return instructions. BAA REV [illegible] Schedule SE (Form 1040) 2017

TAXABLE YEAR FORM

2017 California Resident Income Tax Return 540

APE

ATTACH FEDERAL RETURN

[redacted]-6052 DEUB [redacted] 17 PBA 238990

[redacted]

[redacted] APT 5C

[redacted]

04-05-1967 01-04-1989

1 [ ] Single
4 [ ] Head of household (with qualifying person). See instructions.
2 [X] Married/RDP filing jointly. See inst.
5 [ ] Qualifying widow(er) with dependent child. Enter year spouse/RDP died [ ]
3 [ ] Married/RDP filing separately. Enter spouse's/RDP's SSN or ITIN above and full name here [ ]

If your California filing status is different from your federal filing status, check the box here . . . . [ ]

6 If someone can claim you (or your spouse/RDP) as a dependent, check the box here. See inst . . . . . . 6 [ ]

▶ For line 7, line 8, line 9, and line 10: Multiply the amount you enter in the box by the pre-printed dollar amount for that line. Whole dollars only

7 Personal: If you checked box 1, 3, or 4 above, enter 1 in the box. If you checked box 2 or 5, enter 2 in the box. If you checked the box on line 6, see instructions. 7 [2] X $114 = $ 228

8 Blind: If you (or your spouse/RDP) are visually impaired, enter 1; if both are visually impaired, enter 2 . . . . 8 [ ] X $114 = $

9 Senior: If you (or your spouse/RDP) are 65 or older, enter 1; if both are 65 or older, enter 2 . . . . 9 [ ] X $114 = $

10 Dependents: Do not include yourself or your spouse/RDP.

	Dependent 1	Dependent 2	Dependent 3
First Name			
Last Name			
SSN			
Dependent's relationship to you			

Total dependent exemptions . . . . 10 [ ] X $353 = $

11 Exemption amount: Add line 7 through line 10. Transfer this amount to line 32. . . . . 11 $ 228

Your name: [redacted] Your SSN or ITIN: [redacted]

12	State wages from your Form(s) W-2, box 16	12	.00
13	Enter federal adjusted gross income from Form 1040, line 37; 1040A, line 21; or 1040EZ, line 4	13	2 603 .00
14	California adjustments – subtractions. Enter the amount from Schedule CA (540), line 37, column B	14	.00
15	Subtract line 14 from line 13. If less than zero, enter the result in parentheses. See instructions	15	2603 .00
16	California adjustments – additions. Enter the amount from Schedule CA (540), line 37, column C	16	.00
17	California adjusted gross income. Combine line 15 and line 16	17	2603 .00
18	Enter the larger of: Your California itemized deductions from Schedule CA (540), line 44; OR Your California standard deduction shown below for your filing status: • Single or Married/RDP filing separately ... $4,236 • Married/RDP filing jointly, Head of household, or Qualifying widow(er) ... $8,472. If Married/RDP filing separately or the box on line 6 is checked, STOP. See instructions	18	8472 .00
19	Subtract line 18 from line 17. This is your taxable income. If less than zero, enter -0-	19	0 .00
31	Tax. Check the box if from: [X] Tax Table [ ] Tax Rate Schedule [ ] FTB 3800 [ ] FTB 3803	31	0 .00
32	Exemption credits. Enter the amount from line 11. If your federal AGI is more than $187,203, see instructions	32	228 .00
33	Subtract line 32 from line 31. If less than zero, enter -0-	33	0 .00
34	Tax. See instructions. Check the box if from: [ ] Schedule G-1 [ ] FTB 5870A	34	.00
35	Add line 33 and line 34	35	0 .00
40	Nonrefundable Child and Dependent Care Expenses Credit. See instructions	40	.00
43	Enter credit name ____ code ____ and amount	43	.00
44	Enter credit name ____ code ____ and amount	44	.00
45	To claim more than two credits, see instructions. Attach Schedule P (540)	45	.00
46	Nonrefundable renter's credit. See instructions	46	.00
47	Add line 40 through line 46. These are your total credits	47	.00
48	Subtract line 47 from line 35. If less than zero, enter -0-	48	0 .00
61	Alternative minimum tax. Attach Schedule P (540)	61	.00
62	Mental Health Services Tax. See instructions	62	.00
63	Other taxes and credit recapture. See instructions	63	.00
64	Add line 48, line 61, line 62, and line 63. This is your total tax	64	0 .00

Your name: [redacted] Your SSN or ITIN: [redacted]

71	California income tax withheld. See instructions	71	.00
72	2017 CA estimated tax and other payments. See instructions	72	.00
73	Withholding (Form 592-B and/or 593). See instructions	73	.00
74	Excess SDI (or VPDI) withheld. See instructions	74	.00
75	Earned Income Tax Credit (EITC)	75	.00
76	Add lines 71 through 75. These are your total payments. See instructions	76	.00

91	Use Tax. Do not leave blank. See instructions	91	0 .00

If line 91 is zero, check if:

[X] No use tax is owed.

[ ] You paid your use tax obligation directly to CDTFA.

92	Payments balance. If line 76 is more than line 91, subtract line 91 from line 76	92	.00
93	Use Tax balance. If line 91 is more than line 76, subtract line 76 from line 91	93	.00
94	Overpaid tax. If line 92 is more than line 64, subtract line 64 from line 92	94	.00
95	Amount of line 94 you want applied to your 2018 estimated tax	95	.00
96	Overpaid tax available this year. Subtract line 95 from line 94	96	.00
97	Tax due. If line 92 is less than line 64, subtract line 92 from line 64	97	0 .00

Your name: [redacted] Your SSN or ITIN: [redacted]

Contributions

	Code	Amount
California Seniors Special Fund. See instructions	400	.00
Alzheimer's Disease/Related Disorders Fund	401	.00
Rare and [redacted] Species Preservation Voluntary Tax Contribution Program	403	.00
California Breast Cancer Research Voluntary Tax Contribution Fund	405	.00
California Firefighters' Memorial Fund	406	.00
Emergency Food for Families Voluntary Tax Contribution Fund	407	.00
California Peace Officer Memorial Foundation Fund	408	.00
California Sea Otter Fund	410	.00
California Cancer Research Voluntary Tax Contribution Fund	413	.00
School Supplies for Homeless Children Fund	422	.00
State Parks Protection Fund/Parks Pass Purchase	423	.00
Protect Our Coast and Oceans Voluntary Tax Contribution Fund	424	.00
Keep Arts in Schools Voluntary Tax Contribution Fund	425	.00
State Children's Trust Fund for the Prevention of Child Abuse	430	.00
Prevention of Animal Homelessness and Cruelty Fund	431	.00
Revive the Salton Sea Fund	432	.00
California Domestic Violence Victims Fund	433	.00
Special Olympics Fund	434	.00
Type 1 Diabetes Research Fund	435	.00
California YMCA Youth and Government Voluntary Tax Contribution Fund	436	.00
Habitat for Humanity Voluntary Tax Contribution Fund	437	.00
California Senior Citizen Advocacy Voluntary Tax Contribution Fund	438	.00
Native California Wildlife Rehabilitation Voluntary Tax Contribution Fund	439	.00
Rape Backlog Kit Voluntary Tax Contribution Fund	440	.00
110 Add code 400 through code 440. This is your total contribution	110	.00

Your name: [redacted] Your SSN or ITIN: [redacted]

111 **AMOUNT YOU OWE.** If you do not have an amount on line 96, add line 93, line 97, and line 110. See instructions. Do not send cash.
Mail to: FRANCHISE TAX BOARD
PO BOX 942867
SACRAMENTO CA 94267-0001 .... 111 .00
Pay online – Go to ftb.ca.gov/pay for more information.

112 Interest, late return penalties, and late payment penalties .... 112 .00

113 Underpayment of estimated tax. Check the box: ☐ FTB 5805 attached ☐ FTB 5805F attached 113 .00

114 Total amount due. See instructions. Enclose, but do not staple, any payment .... 114 .00

115 **REFUND OR NO AMOUNT DUE.** Subtract the sum of line 110, line 112 and line 113 from line 96. See instructions.
Mail to: FRANCHISE TAX BOARD
PO BOX 942840
SACRAMENTO CA 94240-0001 .... 115 0 .00

Fill in the information to authorize direct deposit of your refund into one or two accounts. Do not attach a voided check or a deposit slip. See instructions.
Have you verified the routing and account numbers? Use whole dollars only.
All or the following amount of my refund (line 115) is authorized for direct deposit into the account shown below:

Routing number | Type: ☐ Checking ☐ Savings | Account number | 116 Direct deposit amount .00

The remaining amount of my refund (line 115) is authorized for direct deposit into the account shown below:

Routing number | Type: ☐ Checking ☐ Savings | Account number | 117 Direct deposit amount .00

IMPORTANT: See the instructions to find out if you should attach a copy of your complete federal tax return.

To learn about your privacy rights, how we may use your information, and the consequences for not providing the requested information, go to ftb.ca.gov/forms and search for 1131. To request this notice by mail, call 800.852.5711. Under penalties of perjury, I declare that I have examined this tax return, including accompanying schedules and statements, and to the best of my knowledge and belief, it is true, correct, and complete.

Your signature | Date | Spouse's/RDP's signature (if a joint tax return, both must sign)

Sign Here

It is unlawful to forge a spouse's/RDP's signature.

Joint tax return? (See instructions)

Your email address. Enter only one email address. | Preferred phone number

Paid preparer's signature (declaration of preparer is based on all information of which preparer has any knowledge)
ROLANDO C. NAVARRO

Firm's name (or yours, if self-employed): ROLLY'S TAX SERVICES | PTIN: P 0 0 0 9 1 [illegible] 2 3

Firm's address: 3913 LONG BEACH BLVD LONG BEACH CA 9080[illegible] | FEIN: 2 7 3 5 2 5 6 6 [illegible]

Do you want to allow another person to discuss this tax return with us? See instructions ... ☒ Yes ☐ No

Print Third Party Designee's Name: ROLANDO C NAVARRO | Telephone Number: (562) 490-3711

PAYER'S name, street address, city or town, province or state, country, ZIP or foreign postal code

Victoria Partners DBA Monte Carlo Resort & Casino
3770 Las Vegas Blvd. South
Las Vegas, NV 89109

1 Gross winnings: Slots $1,521.00	2 Date won: 8 3 2017
3 Type of wager: 7	4 Federal income tax withheld: $0.00
5 Transaction: 102590	6 Race: 36773414
7 Winnings from identical wagers	8 Cashier: S. Fein
9 Winner's taxpayer identification no.: 081-54-6032	10 Window: 3
[redacted]	12 Second ID: MD#73445525
13 State/Payer's state identification no.	14 State winnings: $
15 State income tax withheld: $	16 Local winnings: $
17 Local income tax withheld: $	18 Name of locality

Federal identification number: [redacted]
Telephone number: (702) 730-7777

WINNER'S name, address (including apt. no.), and ZIP code: [redacted] G [redacted]

Signature ▸ Date ▸

OMB No. 1545-0 201 Form W-2 Certa Gambli Winni

Copy

Report this income on y federal tax return. If form shows federal inc tax withheld in box 4, at this copy to your ret

Form W-2G www.irs.gov/w2g Department of the Treasury - Internal Revenue Servi

☐ VOID ☐ CORRECTED (if checked)

PAYER'S name, street address, city or town, province or state, country, ZIP or foreign postal code

Victoria Partners DBA Monte Carlo Resort & Casino
3770 Las Vegas Blvd. South
Las Vegas, NV 89109

1 Gross winnings: Slots $1,521.00	2 Date won: 8 3 2017
3 Type of wager: 7	4 Federal income tax withheld: $0.00
5 Transaction: 102590	6 Race: 36773414
7 Winnings from identical wagers	8 Cashier: S. Fein
9 Winner's taxpayer identification no.: 081-54-6032	10 Window: 3
11 First I.D.: F1780306	12 Second ID: MD#73445525
13 State/Payer's state identification no.	14 State winnings: $
15 State income tax withheld: $	16 Local winnings: $
17 Local income tax withheld: $	18 Name of locality

Federal identification number: [redacted]
Telephone number: (702) 730-7777

WINNER'S name, address (including apt. no.), and ZIP code: [redacted] G [redacted]

Signature ▸ Date ▸

OMB No. 1545-0 201 Form W-2 Certa Gambli Winni

This is important tax inform and is being furnished t Internal Revenue Serv

Copy For Winner's Rec

Form W-2G www.irs.gov/w2g Department of the Treasury - Internal Revenue Serv

Exhibit '4'

Copy of the Birth Certificate of the Beneficiary

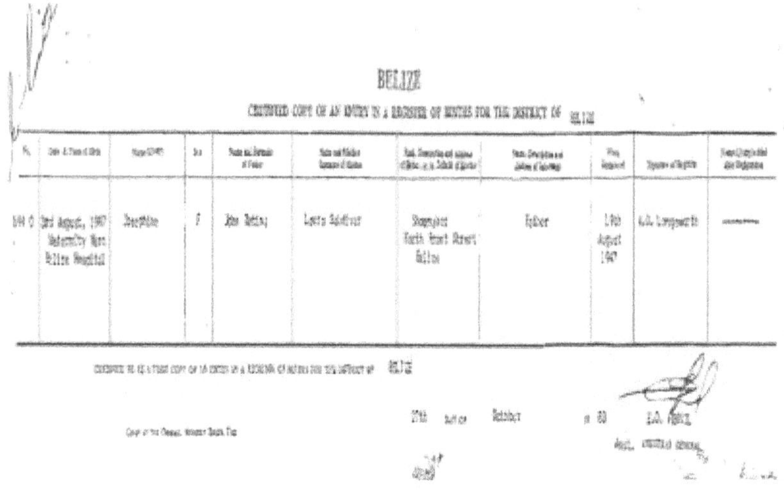

BELIZE

CERTIFIED COPY OF AN ENTRY IN A REGISTER OF BIRTHS FOR THE DISTRICT OF BELIZE

3rd August, 1947

19th August 1947

Exhibit '5'

Copy of the I-194, Passport and Visa of the Beneficiary

Departure Number

589690521 11

Immigration and Naturalization Service

I-94

Departure Record

ADMITTED

LAX

MAR 3 0 2005

B-2

SEP 2 9 2005

14. Family Name

[redacted]

15. First (Given) Name

[redacted]

16. Birth Date (Day/Mo/Yr)

[redacted]

17. Country of Citizenship

[redacted]

See Other Side

STAPLE HERE

REPUBLIKA NG PILIPINAS
REPUBLIC OF THE PHILIPPINES
Kagawaran ng Ugnayang Panlabas
Department of Foreign Affairs

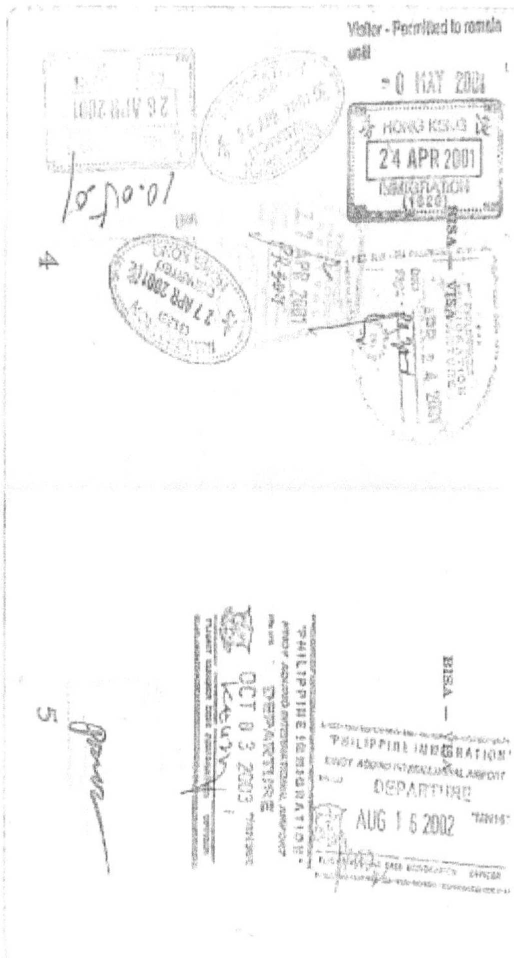
Visitor - Permitted to remain until
HONG KONG
24 APR 2001
IMMIGRATION
4
PHILIPPINE IMMIGRATION
DEPARTURE
5

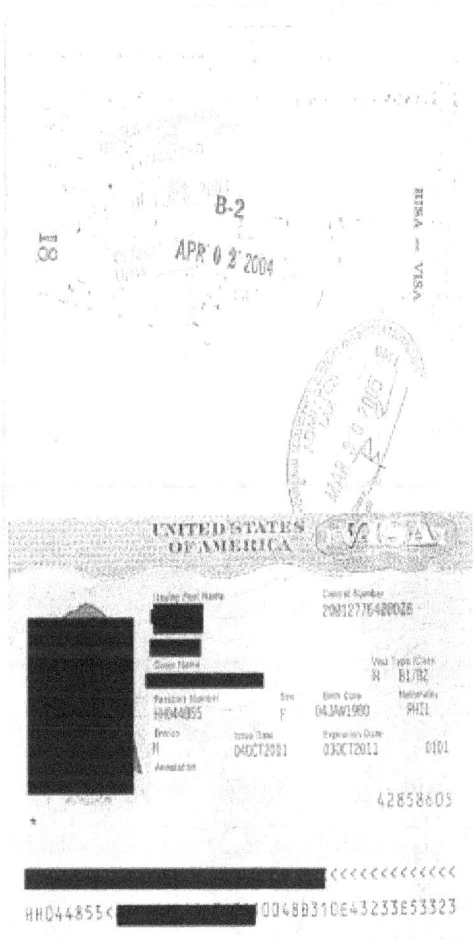
B-2
APR 0 2 2004
VISA
UNITED STATES
OF AMERICA
VISA

Exhibit '6'
2017 Tax Return and W-2 Form of the Co-Sponsor

Form **1040** Department of the Treasury—Internal Revenue Service (99) **U.S. Individual Income Tax Return** **2017** OMB No. 1545-0074 IRS Use Only—Do not write or staple in this space.

For the year Jan. 1–Dec. 31, 2017, or other tax year beginning , 2017, ending , 20 | See separate instructions.

Your first name and initial CHARINA	Last name JOHNSON	Your social security number [redacted]
If a joint return, spouse's first name and initial JASON	Last name JOHNSON	Spouse's social security number [redacted]
Home address (number and street). If you have a P.O. box, see instructions. [redacted]	Apt. no.	Make sure the SSN(s) above and on line 6c are correct.
City, town or post office, state, and ZIP code. If you have a foreign address, also complete spaces below (see instructions). [redacted]		Presidential Election Campaign Check here if you, or your spouse if filing jointly, want $3 to go to this fund. Checking a box below will not change your tax or refund. ☒ You ☒ Spouse
Foreign country name	Foreign province/state/county	Foreign postal code

Filing Status

Check only one box.

1 ☐ Single
2 ☒ Married filing jointly (even if only one had income)
3 ☐ Married filing separately. Enter spouse's SSN above and full name here. ▶
4 ☐ Head of household (with qualifying person). (See instructions.) If the qualifying person is a child but not your [redacted] enter this child's name here. ▶
5 ☐ Qualifying widow(er) (see instructions)

Exemptions

6a ☒ Yourself. If someone can claim you as a dependent, do not check box 6a
b ☒ Spouse

Boxes checked on 6a and 6b: 2

c Dependents:

(1) First name	Last name	(2) Dependent's social security number	(3) Dependent's relationship to you	(4) ✓ if child under age 17 qualifying for child tax credit (see instructions)
DAVID	JOHNSON	605-43-8774	Son	☒
SALVADOR	VALERIO	605-51-0884	Son	☐
				☐
				☐

If more than four dependents, see instructions and check here ▶☐

No. of children on 6c who: • lived with you: 2
• did not live with you due to divorce or separation (see instructions)
Dependents on 6c not entered above
Add numbers on lines above ▶ 4

d Total number of exemptions claimed

Income

Attach Form(s) W-2 here. Also attach Forms W-2G and 1099-R if tax was withheld.

If you did not get a W-2, see instructions.

7	Wages, salaries, tips, etc. Attach Form(s) W-2	7	156,022.
8a	Taxable interest. Attach Schedule B if required	8a	21.
b	Tax-exempt interest. Do not include on line 8a — 8b		
9a	Ordinary dividends. Attach Schedule B if required	9a	
b	Qualified dividends — 9b		
10	Taxable refunds, credits, or offsets of state and local income taxes	10	1,806.
11	Alimony received	11	
12	Business income or (loss). Attach Schedule C or C-EZ	12	-9,969.
13	Capital gain or (loss). Attach Schedule D if required. If not required, check here ▶ ☐	13	
14	Other gains or (losses). Attach Form 4797	14	
15a	IRA distributions 15a — b Taxable amount	15b	
16a	Pensions and annuities 16a — b Taxable amount	16b	
17	Rental real estate, royalties, partnerships, S corporations, trusts, etc. Attach Schedule E	17	
18	Farm income or (loss). Attach Schedule F	18	
19	Unemployment compensation	19	
20a	Social security benefits 20a — b Taxable amount	20b	
21	Other income. List type and amount	21	
22	Combine the amounts in the far right column for lines 7 through 21. This is your total income ▶	22	148,080.

Adjusted Gross Income

23	Educator expenses	23	
24	Certain business expenses of reservists, performing artists, and fee-basis government officials. Attach Form 2106 or 2106-EZ	24	
25	Health savings account deduction. Attach Form 8889	25	
26	Moving expenses. Attach Form 3903	26	
27	Deductible part of self-employment tax. Attach Schedule SE	27	
28	Self-employed SEP, SIMPLE, and qualified plans	28	
29	Self-employed health insurance deduction	29	
30	Penalty on early withdrawal of savings	30	
31a	Alimony paid b Recipient's SSN ▶	31a	
32	IRA deduction	32	
33	Student loan interest deduction	33	
34	Reserved for future use	34	
35	Domestic production activities deduction. Attach Form 8903	35	

Form 1040 (2017) Page 2

Tax and Credits	38	Amount from line 37 (adjusted gross income)			38	140,680.
	39a	Check if: ☐ You were born before January 2, 1953, ☐ Blind. ☐ Spouse was born before January 2, 1953, ☐ Blind. Total boxes checked ▶ 39a				
	b	If your spouse itemizes on a separate return or you were a dual-status alien, check here ▶ 39b ☐				
Standard Deduction for— • People who check any box on line 39a or 39b or who can be claimed as a dependent, see instructions. • All others: Single or Married filing separately, $6,350; Married filing jointly or Qualifying widow(er), $12,700; Head of household, $9,350	40	Itemized deductions (from Schedule A) or your standard deduction (see left margin)			40	41,980.
	41	Subtract line 40 from line 38			41	106,700.
	42	Exemptions. If line 38 is $156,900 or less, multiply $4,050 by the number on line 6d. Otherwise, see instructions			42	16,200.
	43	Taxable income. Subtract line 42 from line 41. If line 42 is more than line 41, enter -0-			43	90,500.
	44	Tax (see instructions). Check if any from: a ☐ Form(s) 8814 b ☐ Form 4972 c ☐			44	14,109.
	45	Alternative minimum tax (see instructions). Attach Form 6251			45	
	46	Excess advance premium tax credit repayment. Attach Form 8962			46	
	47	Add lines 44, 45, and 46 ▶			47	14,109.
	48	Foreign tax credit. Attach Form 1116 if required	48			
	49	Credit for child and dependent care expenses. Attach Form 2441	49			
	50	Education credits from Form 8863, line 19	50			
	51	Retirement savings contributions credit. Attach Form 8880	51			
	52	Child tax credit. Attach Schedule 8812, if required	52			
	53	Residential energy credit. Attach Form 5695	53			
	54	Other credits from Form: a ☐ 3800 b ☐ 8801 c ☐	54			
	55	Add lines 48 through 54. These are your total credits			55	
	56	Subtract line 55 from line 47. If line 55 is more than line 47, enter -0- ▶			56	14,109.
Other Taxes	57	Self-employment tax. Attach Schedule SE			57	
	58	Unreported social security and Medicare tax from Form: a ☐ 4137 b ☐ 8919			58	
	59	Additional tax on IRAs, other qualified retirement plans, etc. Attach Form 5329 if required			59	
	60a	Household employment taxes from Schedule H			60a	
	b	First-time homebuyer credit repayment. Attach Form 5405 if required			60b	
	61	Health care: individual responsibility (see instructions) Full-year coverage ☒			61	
	62	Taxes from: a ☐ Form 8959 b ☐ Form 8960 c ☐ Instructions; enter code(s)			62	
	63	Add lines 56 through 62. This is your total tax ▶			63	14,109.
Payments	64	Federal income tax withheld from Forms W-2 and 1099	64	18,265.		
If you have a qualifying child, attach Schedule EIC.	65	2017 estimated tax payments and amount applied from 2016 return	65			
	66a	Earned income credit (EIC) No	66a			
	b	Nontaxable combat pay election 66b				
	67	Additional child tax credit. Attach Schedule 8812	67			
	68	American opportunity credit from Form 8863, line 8	68			
	69	Net premium tax credit. Attach Form 8962	69			
	70	Amount paid with request for extension to file	70			
	71	Excess social security and tier 1 RRTA tax withheld	71			
	72	Credit for federal tax on fuels. Attach Form 4136	72			
	73	Credits from Form: a ☐ 2439 b ☐ Reserved c ☐ 8885 d ☐	73			
	74	Add lines 64, 65, 66a, and 67 through 73. These are your total payments ▶			74	18,265.
Refund	75	If line 74 is more than line 63, subtract line 63 from line 74. This is the amount you overpaid			75	4,156.
	76a	Amount of line 75 you want refunded to you. If Form 8888 is attached, check here ▶ ☐			76a	4,156.
Direct deposit? See instructions.	b	Routing number 1 2 2 2 3 5 8 2 1 ▶ c Type: ☒ Checking ☐ Savings				
	d	Account number 1 5 7 5 0 9 6 5 6 8 5 4				
	77	Amount of line 75 you want applied to your 2018 estimated tax ▶	77			
Amount You Owe	78	Amount you owe. Subtract line 74 from line 63. For details on how to pay, see instructions ▶			78	
	79	Estimated tax penalty (see instructions)	79			

Third Party Designee Do you want to allow another person to discuss this return with the IRS (see instructions)? ☐ Yes. Complete below. ☒ No

Designee's name ▶ Phone no. ▶ Personal identification number (PIN) ▶

Sign Here Under penalties of perjury, I declare that I have examined this return and accompanying schedules and statements, and to the best of my knowledge and belief, they are true, correct, and accurately list all amounts and sources of income I received during the tax year. Declaration of preparer (other than taxpayer) is based on all information of which preparer has any knowledge.

Joint return? See instructions. Keep a copy for your records.

Your signature	Date	Your occupation	Daytime phone number
		REGISTERED NURSE	(909)821-4657
Spouse's signature. If a joint return, both must sign.	Date	Spouse's occupation	If the IRS sent you an Identity Protection PIN, enter it here (see inst.)
		TEACHER	

Paid Preparer Use

Print/Type preparer's name	Preparer's signature	Date	Check ☐ if self-employed	PTIN
	Self-Prepared			

SCHEDULE A (Form 1040)
Department of the Treasury Internal Revenue Service (99)

Itemized Deductions

▶ Go to www.irs.gov/ScheduleA for instructions and the latest information.
▶ Attach to Form 1040.
Caution: If you are claiming a net qualified disaster loss on Form 4684, see the instructions for line 28.

OMB No. 1545-0074
2017
Attachment Sequence No. 07

Name(s) shown on Form 1040: CHARINA & JASON JOHNSON
Your social security number: [redacted]

Medical and Dental Expenses		Caution: Do not include expenses reimbursed or paid by others.				
	1	Medical and dental expenses (see instructions)	1	4,000.		
	2	Enter amount from Form 1040, line 38 [2] 148,680.				
	3	Multiply line 2 by 7.5% (0.075)	3	11,151.		
	4	Subtract line 3 from line 1. If line 3 is more than line 1, enter -0-			4	0.
Taxes You Paid	5	State and local (check only one box): a [X] Income taxes, or b [ ] General sales taxes	5	6,698.		
	6	Real estate taxes (see instructions)	6	5,318.		
	7	Personal property taxes	7			
	8	Other taxes. List type and amount ▶ See Schedule A, Line 8 Statement	8	830.		
	9	Add lines 5 through 8			9	12,846.
Interest You Paid	10	Home mortgage interest and points reported to you on Form 1098	10	13,024.		
Note: Your mortgage interest deduction may be limited (see instructions).	11	Home mortgage interest not reported to you on Form 1098. If paid to the person from whom you bought the home, see instructions and show that person's name, identifying no., and address ▶	11			
	12	Points not reported to you on Form 1098. See instructions for special rules	12			
	13	Reserved for future use	13			
	14	Investment interest. Attach Form 4952 if required. See instructions	14			
	15	Add lines 10 through 14			15	13,024.
Gifts to Charity	16	Gifts by cash or check. If you made any gift of $250 or more, see instructions	16	12,000.		
If you made a gift and got a benefit for it, see instructions.	17	Other than by cash or check. If any gift of $250 or more, see instructions. You must attach Form 8283 if over $500	17	250.		
	18	Carryover from prior year	18			
	19	Add lines 16 through 18			19	12,250.
Casualty and Theft Losses	20	Casualty or theft loss(es) other than net qualified disaster losses. Attach Form 4684 and enter the amount from line 18 of that form. See instructions			20	
Job Expenses and Certain Miscellaneous Deductions	21	Unreimbursed employee expenses—job travel, union dues, job education, etc. Attach Form 2106 or 2106-EZ if required. See instructions. ▶ See Schedule A, Line 21 Statement	21	5,133.		
	22	Tax preparation fees	22	275.		
	23	Other expenses—investment, safe deposit box, etc. List type and amount ▶ See Schedule A, Line 23 Statement	23	1,426.		
	24	Add lines 21 through 23	24	6,834.		
	25	Enter amount from Form 1040, line 38 [25] 148,680.				
	26	Multiply line 25 by 2% (0.02)	26	2,974.		
	27	Subtract line 26 from line 24. If line 26 is more than line 24, enter -0-			27	3,860.
Other Miscellaneous Deductions	28	Other—from list in instructions. List type and amount ▶			28	
Total Itemized Deductions	29	Is Form 1040, line 38, over $156,900? [X] No. Your deduction is not limited. Add the amounts in the far right column for lines 4 through 28. Also, enter this amount on Form 1040, line 40. [ ] Yes. Your deduction may be limited. See the Itemized Deductions Worksheet in the instructions to figure the amount to enter.			29	41,980.
	30	If you elect to itemize deductions even though they are less than your standard				

SCHEDULE C (Form 1040) — Department of the Treasury, Internal Revenue Service (99)

Profit or Loss From Business
(Sole Proprietorship)

▶ Go to www.irs.gov/ScheduleC for instructions and the latest information.
▶ Attach to Form 1040, 1040NR, or 1041; partnerships generally must file Form 1065.

OMB No. 1545-0074 — **2017** — Attachment Sequence No. 09

Name of proprietor: JASON JOHNSON — Social security number (SSN): [redacted]

A Principal business or profession, including product or service (see instructions): ALL OTHER PROFESSION
B Enter code from instructions ▶ 5 4 1 9 9 0
C Business name. If no separate business name, leave blank: JJ AIR CONDITIONING & HEATING
D Employer ID number (EIN) (see instr.)
E Business address (including suite or room no.) ▶ 861 SAPPHIRE CT
City, town or post office, state, and ZIP code: POMONA, CA 91766
F Accounting method: (1) ☒ Cash (2) ☐ Accrual (3) ☐ Other (specify) ▶
G Did you "materially participate" in the operation of this business during 2017? If "No," see instructions for limit on losses . ☒ Yes ☐ No
H If you started or acquired this business during 2017, check here ▶ ☐
I Did you make any payments in 2017 that would require you to file Form(s) 1099? (see instructions) ☐ Yes ☒ No
J If "Yes," did you or will you file required Forms 1099? ☐ Yes ☐ No

Part I Income

1	Gross receipts or sales. See instructions for line 1 and check the box if this income was reported to you on Form W-2 and the "Statutory employee" box on that form was checked ▶ ☐	1	9,300.
2	Returns and allowances	2	
3	Subtract line 2 from line 1	3	9,300.
4	Cost of goods sold (from line 42)	4	
5	Gross profit. Subtract line 4 from line 3	5	9,300.
6	Other income, including federal and state gasoline or fuel tax credit or refund (see instructions)	6	
7	Gross income. Add lines 5 and 6 ▶	7	9,300.

Part II Expenses. Enter expenses for business use of your home only on line 30.

		Line	Amount			Line	Amount
8	Advertising	8	3,007.	18	Office expense (see instructions)	18	
9	Car and truck expenses (see instructions)	9	1,736.	19	Pension and profit-sharing plans	19	
10	Commissions and fees	10		20	Rent or lease (see instructions):		
11	Contract labor (see instructions)	11		a	Vehicles, machinery, and equipment	20a	
12	Depletion	12		b	Other business property	20b	
13	Depreciation and section 179 expense deduction (not included in Part III) (see instructions)	13		21	Repairs and maintenance	21	
14	Employee benefit programs (other than on line 19)	14		22	Supplies (not included in Part III)	22	1,254.
15	Insurance (other than health)	15		23	Taxes and licenses	23	
16	Interest:			24	Travel, meals, and entertainment:		
a	Mortgage (paid to banks, etc.)	16a		a	Travel	24a	
b	Other	16b		b	Deductible meals and entertainment (see instructions)	24b	300.
17	Legal and professional services	17	250.	25	Utilities	25	1,242.
				26	Wages (less employment credits)	26	
				27a	Other expenses (from line 48)	27a	11,480.
				b	Reserved for future use	27b	

28	Total expenses before expenses for business use of home. Add lines 8 through 27a ▶	28	19,269.
29	Tentative profit or (loss). Subtract line 28 from line 7	29	-9,969.
30	Expenses for business use of your home. Do not report these expenses elsewhere. Attach Form 8829 unless using the simplified method (see instructions). Simplified method filers only: enter the total square footage of: (a) your home: ______ and (b) the part of your home used for business: ______ Use the Simplified Method Worksheet in the instructions to figure the amount to enter on line 30	30	
31	Net profit or (loss). Subtract line 30 from line 29. • If a profit, enter on both Form 1040, line 12 (or Form 1040NR, line 13) and on Schedule SE, line 2. (If you checked the box on line 1, see instructions). Estates and trusts, enter on Form 1041, line 3. • If a loss, you must go to line 32.	31	-9,969.

32 If you have a loss, check the box that describes your investment in this activity (see instructions).
• If you checked 32a, enter the loss on both Form 1040, line 12, (or Form 1040NR, line 13) and on Schedule SE, line 2. (If you checked the box on line 1, see the line 31 instructions). Estates and trusts, enter on Form 1041, line 3.
32a ☒ All investment is at risk.
32b ☐ Some investment is not at risk.

Schedule C (Form 1040) 2017 Page 2

Part III Cost of Goods Sold (see instructions)

33 Method(s) used to value closing inventory: a ☐ Cost b ☐ Lower of cost or market c ☐ Other (attach explanation)

34 Was there any change in determining quantities, costs, or valuations between opening and closing inventory? If "Yes," attach explanation . . . ☐ Yes ☐ No

35 Inventory at beginning of year. If different from last year's closing inventory, attach explanation	35	
36 Purchases less cost of items withdrawn for personal use	36	
37 Cost of labor. Do not include any amounts paid to yourself	37	
38 Materials and supplies	38	
39 Other costs	39	
40 Add lines 35 through 39	40	
41 Inventory at end of year	41	
42 Cost of goods sold. Subtract line 41 from line 40. Enter the result here and on line 4	42	

Part IV Information on Your Vehicle. Complete this part only if you are claiming car or truck expenses on line 9 and are not required to file Form 4562 for this business. See the instructions for line 13 to find out if you must file Form 4562.

43 When did you place your vehicle in service for business purposes? (month, day, year) ▶ 01/01/2012

44 Of the total number of miles you drove your vehicle during 2017, enter the number of miles you used your vehicle for:

a Business 3,245 b Commuting (see instructions) 5,200 c Other 8,007

45 Was your vehicle available for personal use during off-duty hours? . . . ☒ Yes ☐ No

46 Do you (or your spouse) have another vehicle available for personal use? . . . ☒ Yes ☐ No

47a Do you have evidence to support your deduction? . . . ☒ Yes ☐ No

b If "Yes," is the evidence written? . . . ☒ Yes ☐ No

Part V Other Expenses. List below business expenses not included on lines 8–26 or line 30.

PHONE AND CELL EXPENSE	3,795.
SAFETY SHOES	350.
BOND	1,335.
SMALL JOB TOOLS AND RELATED EQUIPMENT	6,000.

CHARINA & JASON JOHNSON [illegible]

Additional information from your 2017 Federal Tax Return

Schedule A: Itemized Deductions
Ln 6a, RE tax main res — Itemization Statement

Description	Amount
SUN WEST MORTGAGE	5,318.
Total	5,318.

Schedule A: Itemized Deductions
Line 8 - Other Taxes — Continuation Statement

Type of Other Deductible Tax	Amount
DMV 2007 MAZDA	150.
DMV 2003 CHEVY	200.
DMV 1999 HONDA	140.
DMV 1974 G30	200.
DMV 1955 F100	140.
Total	830.

Schedule A: Itemized Deductions
Line 21 - Employee Business Expenses Subject to 2% Limitation — Continuation Statement

Description	Amount
Union and professional dues	1,440.
Professional Subscriptions	248.
Uniforms and protective clothing	1,200.
Job search costs	520.
DRY CLEANING	400.
NURSING SHOES AND EQUIPT	1,325.
Total	5,133.

Schedule A: Itemized Deductions
Line 23 - Miscellaneous Expenses Subject to 2% Limitation — Continuation Statement

Type Of Other Miscellaneous Expenses	Amount
PHONE AND CELL EXPENSE	1,000.
CON'T EDUCATION	426.
Total	1,426.

Schedule C (ALL OTHER PROFESSION): Profit or Loss from Business
Ln 1a: Other receipts — Itemization Statement

Description	Amount
GROSS INCOME	9,300.
Total	9,300.

CHARINA & JASON JOHNSON [illegible] [illegible]

Schedule C (ALL OTHER PROFESSION): Profit or Loss from Business

Line 8 Itemization Statement

Description	Amount
YELLOW PAGES ADVERTISING	2,232.
EL CLASSIFICADO ADVERTISING	775.
Total	3,007.

TAXABLE YEAR

2017 California Resident Income Tax Return

FORM 540

APE

ATTACH FEDERAL RETURN

[redacted] JOHN [redacted]

17 PBA 541990

CHARINA JOHNSON

JASON JOHNSON

861 SAPPHIRE CT

POMONA CA 91766

07-12-1960 09-25-1975

1 [ ] Single

2 [X] Married/RDP filing jointly. See inst.

3 [ ] Married/RDP filing separately. Enter spouse's/RDP's SSN or ITIN above and full name here

4 [ ] Head of household (with qualifying person). See instructions.

5 [ ] Qualifying widow(er) with dependent child. Enter year spouse/RDP died

If your California filing status is different from your federal filing status, check the box here . . . . [ ]

6 If someone can claim you (or your spouse/RDP) as a dependent, check the box here. See inst. . . . . . . ● 6 [ ]

▶ For line 7, line 8, line 9, and line 10: Multiply the amount you enter in the box by the pre-printed dollar amount for that line. Whole dollars only

7 Personal: If you checked box 1, 3, or 4 above, enter 1 in the box. If you checked box 2 or 5, enter 2 in the box. If you checked the box on line 6, see instructions. . . ● 7 [2] X $114 = ● $ 228

8 Blind: If you (or your spouse/RDP) are visually impaired, enter 1; if both are visually impaired, enter 2 . . . . ● 8 [ ] X $114 = ● $

9 Senior: If you (or your spouse/RDP) are 65 or older, enter 1; if both are 65 or older, enter 2 . . . . ● 9 [ ] X $114 = ● $

10 Dependents: Do not include yourself or your spouse/RDP.

	Dependent 1	Dependent 2	Dependent 3
First Name	[redacted]	SALVADOR	
Last Name	JOHNSON	VALERIO	
SSN	[redacted]	[redacted]	
Dependent's relationship to you	SON	SON	

Total dependent exemptions . . . . ● 10 [2] X $353 = ● $ 706

11 Exemption amount: Add line 7 through line 10. Transfer this amount to line 32. . . . . ● 11 $ 934

Your name: J O H N S O N Your SSN or ITIN: [redacted]

12	[illegible]	12	[illegible] .00
13	Enter federal adjusted gross income from Form 1040, line 37; 1040A, line 21; or 1040EZ, line 4	13	140660 .00
14	California adjustments – subtractions. Enter the amount from Schedule CA (540), line 37, column B	14	1806 .00
15	Subtract line 14 from line 13. If less than zero, enter the result in parentheses. See instructions	15	140074 .00
16	California adjustments – additions. Enter the amount from Schedule CA (540), line 37, column C	16	.00
17	California adjusted gross income. Combine line 15 and line 16	17	140074 .00
18	Enter the larger of: Your California itemized deductions from Schedule CA (540), line 44; OR Your California standard deduction shown below for your filing status: • Single or Married/RDP filing separately ... $4,236 • Married/RDP filing jointly, Head of household, or Qualifying widow(er) ... $8,472. If Married/RDP filing separately or the box on line 6 is checked, STOP. See instructions	18	35282 .00
19	Subtract line 18 from line 17. This is your taxable income. If less than zero, enter -0-	19	111592 .00
31	Tax. Check the box if from: ☐ Tax Table ☒ Tax Rate Schedule ☐ FTB 3800 ☐ FTB 3803	31	5091 .00
32	Exemption credits. Enter the amount from line 11. If your federal AGI is more than $187,203, see instructions	32	934 .00
33	Subtract line 32 from line 31. If less than zero, enter -0-	33	4157 .00
34	Tax. See instructions. Check the box if from: ☐ Schedule G-1 ☐ FTB 5870A	34	.00
35	Add line 33 and line 34	35	4157 .00
40	Nonrefundable Child and Dependent Care Expenses Credit. See instructions	40	.00
43	Enter credit name ____ code ____ and amount	43	.00
44	Enter credit name ____ code ____ and amount	44	.00
45	To claim more than two credits, see instructions. Attach Schedule P (540)	45	.00
46	Nonrefundable renter's credit. See instructions	46	.00
47	Add line 40 through line 46. These are your total credits	47	.00
48	Subtract line 47 from line 35. If less than zero, enter -0-	48	4157 .00
61	Alternative minimum tax. Attach Schedule P (540)	61	.00
62	Mental Health Services Tax. See instructions	62	.00
63	Other taxes and credit recapture. See instructions	63	.00
64	Add line 48, line 61, line 62, and line 63. This is your total tax	64	4157 .00

Your name: J O H N S O N. Your SSN or ITIN: [redacted]

71	California income tax withheld. See instructions	71	5218 .00
72	2017 CA estimated tax and other payments. See instructions	72	.00
73	Withholding (Form 592-B and/or 593). See instructions	73	.00
74	Excess SDI (or VPDI) withheld. See instructions	74	.00
75	Earned Income Tax Credit (EITC)	75	.00
76	Add lines 71 through 75. These are your total payments. See instructions	76	5218 .00

91	Use Tax. Do not leave blank. See instructions	91	0 .00

If line 91 is zero, check if: [X] No use tax is owed.
[ ] You paid your use tax obligation directly to CDTFA.

92	Payments balance. If line 76 is more than line 91, subtract line 91 from line 76	92	5218 .00
93	Use Tax balance. If line 91 is more than line 76, subtract line 76 from line 91	93	.00
94	Overpaid tax. If line 92 is more than line 64, subtract line 64 from line 92	94	1061 .00
95	Amount of line 94 you want applied to your 2018 estimated tax	95	0 .00
96	Overpaid tax available this year. Subtract line 95 from line 94	96	1061 .00
97	Tax due. If line 92 is less than line 64, subtract line 92 from line 64	97	.00

Your name: J O H N S O N   Your SSN or ITIN [redacted]

Contributions

	Code	Amount
California Seniors Special Fund. See instructions	400	.00
Alzheimer's Disease/Related Disorders Fund	401	.00
Rare and [redacted] Species Preservation Voluntary Tax Contribution Program	403	.00
California Breast Cancer Research Voluntary Tax Contribution Fund	405	.00
California Firefighters' Memorial Fund	406	.00
Emergency Food for Families Voluntary Tax Contribution Fund	407	.00
California Peace Officer Memorial Foundation Fund	408	.00
California Sea Otter Fund	410	.00
California Cancer Research Voluntary Tax Contribution Fund	413	.00
School Supplies for Homeless Children Fund	422	.00
State Parks Protection Fund/Parks Pass Purchase	423	.00
Protect Our Coast and Oceans Voluntary Tax Contribution Fund	424	.00
Keep Arts in Schools Voluntary Tax Contribution Fund	425	.00
State Children's Trust Fund for the Prevention of Child Abuse	430	.00
Prevention of Animal Homelessness and Cruelty Fund	431	.00
Revive the Salton Sea Fund	432	.00
California Domestic Violence Victims Fund	433	.00
Special Olympics Fund	434	.00
Type 1 Diabetes Research Fund	435	.00
California YMCA Youth and Government Voluntary Tax Contribution Fund	436	.00
Habitat for Humanity Voluntary Tax Contribution Fund	437	.00
California Senior Citizen Advocacy Voluntary Tax Contribution Fund	438	.00
Native California Wildlife Rehabilitation Voluntary Tax Contribution Fund	439	.00
Rape Backlog Kit Voluntary Tax Contribution Fund	440	.00
110 Add code 400 through code 440. This is your total contribution	110	.00

Your name: JOHNSON Your SSN or ITIN: [redacted]

111 AMOUNT YOU OWE. If you do not have an amount on line 96, add line 93, line 97, and line 110. See instructions. Do not send cash.
Mail to: FRANCHISE TAX BOARD
PO BOX 942867
SACRAMENTO CA 94267-0001 . . . . 111 [ ] .00
Pay online – Go to ftb.ca.gov/pay for more information.

112 Interest, late return penalties, and late payment penalties . . . . 112 [ ] .00

113 Underpayment of estimated tax. Check the box: [ ] FTB 5805 attached [ ] FTB 5805F attached 113 [ ] .00

114 Total amount due. See instructions. Enclose, but do not staple, any payment. . . . . 114 [ ] .00

115 REFUND OR NO AMOUNT DUE. Subtract the sum of line 110, line 112 and line 113 from line 95. See instructions.
Mail to: FRANCHISE TAX BOARD
PO BOX 942840
SACRAMENTO CA 94240-0001 . . . . 115 1,061 .00

Fill in the information to authorize direct deposit of your refund into one or two accounts. Do not attach a voided check or a deposit slip. See instructions.
Have you verified the routing and account numbers? Use whole dollars only.
All or the following amount of my refund (line 115) is authorized for direct deposit into the account shown below:

Type: [X] Checking [ ] Savings

Routing number: [redacted] Account number: [redacted] 116 Direct deposit amount: 1,061 .00

The remaining amount of my refund (line 115) is authorized for direct deposit into the account shown below:

Type: [ ] Checking [ ] Savings

Routing number: [ ] Account number: [ ] 117 Direct deposit amount: [ ] .00

IMPORTANT: See the instructions to find out if you should attach a copy of your complete federal tax return.

To learn about your privacy rights, how we may use your information, and the consequences for not providing the requested information, go to ftb.ca.gov/forms and search for 1131. To request this notice by mail, call 800.852.5711. Under penalties of perjury, I declare that I have examined this tax return, including accompanying schedules and statements, and to the best of my knowledge and belief, it is true, correct, and complete.

Your signature | Date | Spouse's/RDP's signature (if a joint tax return, both must sign)

Sign Here

It is unlawful to forge a spouse's/RDP's signature.

Joint tax return? (See instructions)

Your email address. Enter only one email address.

Preferred phone number: 9 0 9 8 2 1 4 6 5 7

Paid preparer's signature (declaration of preparer is based on all information of which preparer has any knowledge)
SELF-PREPARED

Firm's name (or yours, if self-employed) | PTIN

Firm's address | FEIN

Do you want to allow another person to discuss this tax return with us? See instructions . . . [ ] Yes [X] No

Print Third Party Designee's Name | Telephone Number

TAXABLE YEAR · CALIFORNIA SCHEDULE

2017 Wage and Tax Statement W-2

Important: Attach this form to the back of your original or amended Form 540, 540 2EZ, or Form 540NR (Long or Short).

Name(s) as shown on tax return: [redacted]

SSN or ITIN: [redacted]

Caution: If this form is filled out, do not send your Form(s) W-2 to the Franchise Tax Board. If your Form(s) W-2 are from multiple states, attach copies showing California tax withheld to this schedule. If this schedule is blank, attach your Form(s) W-2 to the lower front of your tax return. All fields must be completed. DO NOT ATTACH PAYMENT TO THIS SCHEDULE.

*Employee's social security number, name, and address must be the same as the information on the Form(s) W-2.

W-2 Information	1st W-2	2nd W-2
a. Employee's social security number*	[redacted]	[redacted]
b. Employer identification number (EIN)	[redacted]	[redacted]
c. Employer's name	AHMC SAN GABRIEL VALLEY MEDICAL CENTER	WALNUT VALLEY UNIFIED
Address	1000 FREMONT AVE	880 S. LEMON AVE
City	ALHAMBRA	WALNUT
State	CA	CA
Zip code	91803	91789
e. Employee's first name*	[redacted]	[redacted]
Middle initial*		
Last name*	JOHNSON	JOHNSON
Suffix*		
f. Employee address*	861 SAPPHIRE CT	861 SAPPHIRE CT
City*	POMONA	POMONA
State*	CA	CA
Zip code*	91765	91766
1. Wages, tips, other compensation	106,908.	49,834.
2. Federal income tax withheld	10,643.	7,622.
3. Social security wages	115,317.	53,585.
4. Social security tax withheld	7,150.	3,322.
6. Medicare tax withheld	1,672.	777.

W-2 Information	1st W-2		2nd W-2	
7. Social security tips				
8. Allocated tips (not included in box 1)				
10. Dependent care benefits				
11. Nonqualified plans				
12. Codes and amounts	Codes	Amounts	Codes	Amounts
12a.	D	8,329.	DD	17,910.
12b.	DD	14,529.		
12c.				
12d.				
13. Check the appropriate box for: Statutory employee, Retirement plan, or Third-party sick pay	[ ] Statutory employee [X] Retirement plan [ ] Third-party sick pay		[ ] Statutory employee [X] Retirement plan [ ] Third-party sick pay	
14. SDI, VPDI, or CA SDI (from box 14 or 19)	Type: SDI	Amount: 99 8.	Type: SDI-DRD	Amount: 462.
15. State and employer's state ID number	State: CA	Employer's state ID number: 282-0664-7	State: CA	Employer's state ID number: 80094840
16. State wages, tips, etc.	106,980.		49,834.	
17. State income tax	3,276.		1,942.	

REV 12/08/17 PRO

TAXABLE YEAR

SCHEDULE

2017 California Adjustments — Residents CA (540)

Important: Attach this schedule behind Form 540, Side 5 as a supporting California schedule.

Name(s) as shown on tax return: [redacted]

SSN or ITIN: [redacted]

Part I Income Adjustment Schedule

Section A – Income

	Line	A Federal Amounts	B Subtractions	C Additions
7 Wages, salaries, tips, etc. See instructions before making an entry in column B or C	7	156,822.		
8 Taxable interest (b)	8(a)	21.		
9 Ordinary dividends. See instructions. (b)	9(a)			
10 Taxable refunds, credits, offsets of state and local income taxes	10	1,806.	1,806.	
11 Alimony received	11			
12 Business income or (loss)	12	-9,969.		
13 Capital gain or (loss). See instructions	13			
14 Other gains or (losses)	14			
15 IRA distributions. See instructions. (a)	15(b)			
16 Pensions and annuities. See instructions. (a)	16(b)			
17 Rental real estate, royalties, partnerships, S corporations, trusts, etc	17			
18 Farm income or (loss)	18			
19 Unemployment compensation	19			
20 Social security benefits (a)	20(b)			
21 Other income. a California lottery winnings; b Disaster loss deduction from FTB 3805V; c Federal NOL (Form 1040, line 21); d NOL deduction from FTB 3805V; e NOL from FTB 3805Z, 3806, 3807, or 3809; f Other (describe):	21		a b c d e f	a b c d e f
22 Total. Combine line 7 through line 21 in column A. Add line 7 through line 21f in column B and column C. Go to Section B	22	148,680.	1,806.	

Section B – Adjustments to Income

	Line	A	B	C
23 Educator expenses	23			
24 Certain business expenses of reservists, performing artists, and fee-basis government officials	24			
25 Health savings account deduction	25			
26 Moving expenses	26			
27 Deductible part of self-employment tax	27			
28 Self-employed SEP, SIMPLE, and qualified plans	28			
29 Self-employed health insurance deduction	29			
30 Penalty on early withdrawal of savings	30			
31a Alimony paid (b) Recipient's: SSN ___ Last name ___	31a			
32 IRA deduction	32			
33 Student loan interest deduction	33			
34 Reserved	34			
35 Domestic production activities deduction	35			
36 Add line 23 through line 31a and line 32 through line 35 in columns A, B, and C. See instructions	36			
37 Total. Subtract line 36 from line 22 in columns A, B, and C. See instructions	37	148,680.	1,806.	

Part II Adjustments to Federal Itemized Deductions

38 Federal itemized deductions. Enter the amount from federal Schedule A (Form 1040), lines 4, 9, 15, 19, 20, 27, and 28 .... 38 41,980.

39 Enter total of federal Schedule A (Form 1040), line 5 (State Disability Insurance, and state and local income tax, or General Sales Tax) and line 8 (foreign income taxes only). See instructions .... 39 6,698.

40 Subtract line 39 from line 38 .... 40 35,282.

41 Other adjustments including California lottery losses. See instructions. Specify ________ 41

42 Combine line 40 and line 41 .... 42 35,282.

43 Is your federal AGI (Form 540, line 13) more than the amount shown below for your filing status?

Single or married/RDP filing separately $187,203

Head of household $280,808

Married/RDP filing jointly or qualifying widow(er) $374,411

No. Transfer the amount on line 42 to line 43.

Yes. Complete the Itemized Deductions Worksheet in the instructions for Schedule CA (540), line 43 .... 43 35,282.

44 Enter the larger of the amount on line 43 or your standard deduction listed below

Single or married/RDP filing separately. See instructions $4,236

Married/RDP filing jointly, head of household, or qualifying widow(er) $8,472

Transfer the amount on line 44 to Form 540, line 18 .... 44 35,282.

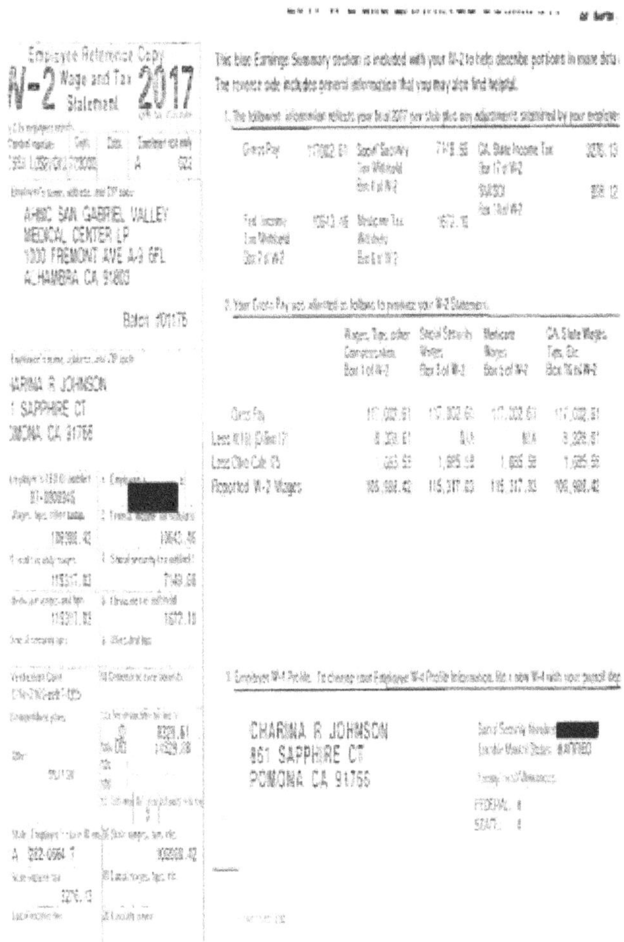
Employee Reference Copy

W-2 Wage and Tax Statement 2017

This blue Earnings Summary section is included with your W-2 to help describe portions in more detail.

The reverse side includes general information that you may also find helpful.

1. The following information reflects your final 2017 pay stub plus any adjustments submitted by your employer.

AHMC SAN GABRIEL VALLEY
MEDICAL CENTER LP
1000 FREMONT AVE A-3 6FL
ALHAMBRA CA 91803

2. Your Gross Pay was adjusted as follows to produce your W-2 Statement.

	Wages, Tips, other Compensation Box 1 of W-2	Social Security Wages Box 3 of W-2	Medicare Wages Box 5 of W-2	CA State Wages, Tips, Etc. Box 16 of W-2
Gross Pay	117,002.61	117,002.61	117,002.61	117,002.61
Less 401(k)	8,328.61	N/A	N/A	8,328.61
Less Other Cafe 125	1,685.58	1,685.58	1,685.58	1,685.58
Reported W-2 Wages	106,988.42	115,317.03	115,317.03	106,988.42

3. Employee W-4 Profile.

CHARINA R JOHNSON
861 SAPPHIRE CT
POMONA CA 91766

Social Security Number [redacted]

Taxable Marital Status: MARRIED

FEDERAL:
STATE:

Employee's SSA number [redacted]

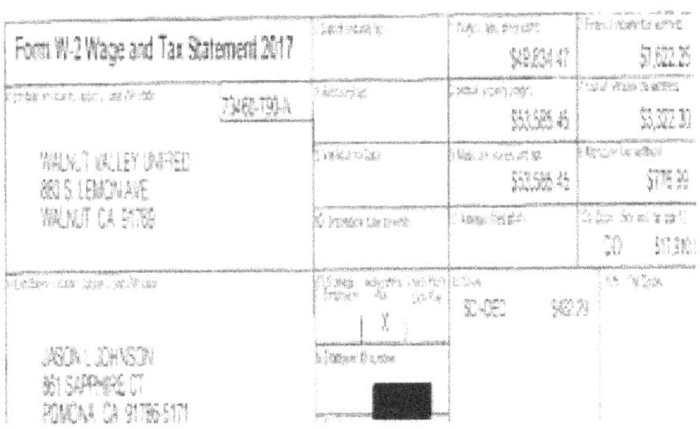
Form W-2 Wage and Tax Statement 2017

WALNUT VALLEY UNIFIED
880 S LEMON AVE
WALNUT CA 91789

Wages, tips, other comp.	$49,834.47
Federal income tax withheld	$7,622.25
Social security wages	$53,585.45
Social security tax withheld	$3,322.30
Medicare wages and tips	$53,585.45
Medicare tax withheld	$776.99

JASON L JOHNSON
861 SAPPHIRE CT
POMONA CA 91766-5171

Employee ID number [redacted]

Exhibit '7'
United States Passport of the Co-Sponsor

PASSPORT
PASSEPORT
PASAPORTE
USA
P
USA
[redacted]
UNITED STATES OF AMERICA
[redacted]
PHILIPPINES
F
18 May 2011
United States
Department of State
17 May 2021
SEE PAGE 27
USA
[redacted]

Exhibit '8'

Employment Verification Letter and Current Paystubs of the Co-Sponsor

San Gabriel Valley Medical Center
AHMC Healthcare

April 2, 2018

To whom it may concern:

This letter is being issued to verify the employment of [redacted]

[redacted], has been employed with San Gabriel Valley Medical Center, AHMC Healthcare, Inc. as of **February 15, 2010** with a current/active employment status as of date of this letter .

If additional information is required please feel free to email at lupe.maravilla@ahmchealth.com

Sincerely,

Lupe Maravilla
Human Resources Generalist
San Gabriel Valley Medical Center
438 W. West Las Tunas Drive
San Gabriel, CA 91776
Direct Line (626) 943-3787

CC: Personnel File

[redacted]

569-0001

AHMC SAN GABRIEL VALLEY
MEDICAL CENTER LP
439 WEST LAS TUNAS DR
SAN GABRIEL, CA 91776

Earnings Statement

ADP

Period Beginning: 05/06/2018
Period Ending: 05/19/2018
Pay Date: 05/25/2018

Taxable Marital Status: Married
Exemptions/Allowances:
Federal: 0
CA: 0

[redacted]

[redacted]

Earnings	rate	hours	this period	year to date
Base Rate	56.9400	68.75	3,914.63	39,453.84
Charge	2.5000	12.00	30.00	545.61
D/T	114.4200	4.00	457.69	1,082.83
Educate	56.9400	2.00	113.88	483.99
Inhouse O/T	85.6800	11.00	942.49	2,249.34
Shift 2	2.0000	8.25	16.50	44.50
Tap	56.9400	1.25	71.18	3,980.13
Overtime				42.83
Education Leav				1,708.20
Inhouse D/T				945.81
	Gross Pay		$5,546.37	50,537.08

Deductions	Statutory	this period	year to date
	Federal Income Tax	-686.05	2,123.11
	Social Security Tax	-339.85	3,089.08
	Medicare Tax	-79.49	722.45
	CA State Income Tax	-269.35	712.20
	CA SUI/SDI Tax	-54.82	498.24
	Other		
	Child Life	-0.69	7.59
	CI Dis/Ad&D	-83.65	920.15
	CI Hspl Cont	-10.06	110.66
	Dental	-58.04*	638.44
	Emp Ad&D	-2.42	26.62
	Emp Life	-10.17	111.87
	Inc Repl	-14.21	156.31
	Sp Ad&D	-2.49	27.39

Other	this period	year to date
Union Cna	-57.79	632.33
Vision	-6.79*	74.69
401-K	-499.17*	4,466.44
401-K Loan	-62.30	685.30
Net Pay	$3,309.03	
Checking	-3,309.03	
Net Check	$0.00	

* Excluded from federal taxable wages

Your federal taxable wages this period are $4,982.37

Other Benefits and Information	this period	total to date
Rsv Sick		134.20
Tap		118.25

Pay Period TAP Breakdown	This Period	Total Taken
Tap Allowed	119.50	
CA Paid Sick Taken	.00	.00
Other TAP Paid	-1.25	
Tap Balance	118.25	
CA Sick Balance		36.00

[redacted]

552-0001

AHMC SAN GABRIEL VALLEY
MEDICAL CENTER LP
438 WEST LAS TUNAS DR
SAN GABRIEL, CA 91776

Taxable Marital Status: Married
Exemptions/Allowances:
Federal: 0
CA: 6

Earnings Statement

ADP

Period Beginning: 05/20/2018
Period Ending: 06/02/2018
Pay Date: 06/08/2018

[redacted]

[redacted]

Earnings	rate	hours	this period	year to date
Base Rate	56.9400	72.00	4,099.68	43,553.52
Hol Diff	28.4700	12.00	341.64	341.64
Inhouse D/T	87.6000	6.00	525.60	2,774.94
Overtime				42.83
Charge				545.61
D/T				1,082.83
Educate				483.99
Education Leav				1,708.20
Inhouse D/T				945.81
Shift 2				44.50
Tap				3,980.13
Gross Pay			$4,966.92	55,504.00

Deductions	Statutory	this period	year to date
	Federal Income Tax	-370.04	2,893.15
	Social Security Tax	-303.93	3,393.01
	Medicare Tax	-71.08	793.53
	CA State Income Tax	-215.40	927.60
	CA SUI/SDI Tax	-49.02	547.26
	Other		
	Child Life	-0.69	8.28
	Cl Dis/Ad&D	-83.65	1,003.80
	Cl Hspl Conf	-10.06	120.72
	Dental	-58.04*	696.48
	Emp Ad&D	-2.42	29.04
	Emp Life	-10.17	122.04
	Inc Repl	-14.21	170.52

Other	this period	year to date
Sp Ad&D	-2.49	29.88
Union Cra	-57.79	690.12
Vision	-6.79*	81.48
401-K	-447.02*	4,913.48
401-K Loan	-62.30	747.60
Net Pay	$3,001.82	
Checking	-3,001.82	
Net Check	$0.00	

* Excluded from federal taxable wages

Your federal taxable wages this period are $4,455.07

Other Benefits and Information	this period	total to date
Rsv Sick		136.05
Tap		127.61

Pay Period TAP Breakdown	This Period	Total Taken
Tap Allowed	127.61	
CA Paid Sick Taken	.00	.00
Other TAP Paid	.00	
Tap Balance	127.61	
CA Sick Balance		36.00

[redacted]

573-0001

AHMC SAN GABRIEL VALLEY
MEDICAL CENTER LP
438 WEST LAS TUNAS DR
SAN GABRIEL, CA 91776

Taxable Marital Status: Married
Exemptions/Allowances:
Federal: 6
CA: 8

Earnings Statement

Period Beginning: 04/22/2018
Period Ending: 05/05/2018
Pay Date: 05/11/2018

[redacted]

[redacted]

Earnings	rate	hours	this period	year to date
Base Rate	56.9400	57.50	3,274.05	35,539.21
Charge	2.5000	34.25	85.62	515.61
Tap	56.9400	14.00	797.16	3,908.95
Overtime				42.83
D/T				625.14
Educate				370.11
Education Leav				1,708.20
Inhouse D/T				945.81
Inhouse O/T				1,306.85
Shift 2				28.00
Gross Pay			$4,156.83	44,990.71

Deductions	Statutory	this period	year to date
	Federal Income Tax	-407.86	1,437.06
	Social Security Tax	-253.70	2,749.23
	Medicare Tax	-59.33	642.96
	CA State Income Tax	-148.54	442.85
	CA SUI/SDI Tax	-40.92	443.42
	Other		
	Child Life	-0.69	6.90
	CI Dis/Ad&D	-83.65	836.50
	CI Hspl Conf	-10.06	100.60
	Dental	-58.04*	580.40
	Emp Ad&D	-2.42	24.20
	Emp Life	-10.17	101.70
	Inc Repl	-14.21	142.10
	Sp Ad&D	-2.49	24.90

Other	this period	year to date
Union Cna	-57.79	574.54
Vision	-6.79*	67.90
401-K	-374.11*	3,967.27
401-K Loan	-62.30	623.00
Net Pay	$2,563.76	
Checking	-2,563.76	
Net Check	$0.00	

* Excluded from federal taxable wages

Your federal taxable wages this period are $3,717.89

Other Benefits and Information	this period	total to date
Rsv Sick		132.35
Tap		110.14

Pay Period TAP Breakdown	This Period	Total Taken
Tap Allowed	124.14	
CA Paid Sick Taken	.00	.00
Other TAP Paid	-14.00	
Tap Balance	110.14	
CA Sick Balance		38.00

Exhibit '9'

Letters of Support from Family and Friends of the Petitioner and the Beneficiary

Roxanne Parker
555 E Silverado Ranch Blvd Unit 2141
Las Vegas, NV 89183
702-690-8072
US Citizen

April 2, 2018

Mary Queen Rivera and Daniel [redacted]
15727 Tetley St. Unit 5C
Hacienda Heights, CA 91745

Dear Officer,

I am writing on behalf of my aunt [redacted] and her husband [redacted] who just recently applied their adjustment of status.

My name is Roxanne Parker and I have known Queenie and Dan for the past 3 years since I'm married to their nephew Ernest King. They are the closest family that we have ever since my husband and I moved here in the United States. I can remember the first time that I met them is when they came and picked Ernest and I from the airport. They were kind enough to stay with us on our 6 hours layover in L.A and drove us around and make sure we ate breakfast before our flight. My husband I spent our first long weekend at their home in California. They were accommodating and kind to us as if we were their own children. They will also spend their holidays and birthdays with us by driving 3 hours from L.A to Vegas where my husband and I currently reside when their schedule permits.

They are both loving and nourishing couple. The most humble people I've ever met. I think they stand as like parents to us. They call us every other week to check up on us and make sure we are okay. Plus, my husband and I look up to them as a couple that we want to be because they really love each other and I can tell how much they mean to each other.

If you have any questions or need further assistance please let me know and get in touch with me using the contact information I provided above. I would be glad to assist in any way that I can.

Sincerely,

Roxanne Parker

Ernest King V. Rivera
555 E Silverado Ranch Blvd Unit 2141
Las Vegas, NV 89183
702-690-8080
Citizen of the Philippines

April 2, 2018

[redacted] Rivera and [redacted]
15727 Tetley St. Unit 5C
Hacienda Heights, CA 91745

Dear Officer,

I am writing on behalf of my aunt [redacted] and her husband [redacted] who just recently applied their adjustment of status.

My name is Ernest King Rivera and I have known Queenie and [redacted] as a couple for the past 7 years. I first met [redacted] personally when I had my first trip here in the United States back in 2014. They have always been accommodating and let me stay with them when I would always come in to fly to LA for my job. When my wife and I have decided to reside here in the united states they helped us with our transition and helped us to adjust with the changes we needed to undergo through. Though my wife and I reside in Las Vegas they always find time to come visit us and check up on how we are doing.

They are an amazing couple that exudes happiness every time you see them. I've seen their relationship grow even stronger as time has pass by and it's something I look up to.

If you have any questions or need further assistance please let me know and get in touch with me using the contact information I provided above. I would be glad to assist in any way that I can.

Sincerely,

Ernest King Rivera

Jeffrey C. [redacted]

2425 Bearskin Ln
Monroe, NC 28110
(704) 290-8637
United States Citizen

May 3, 2018

Re: [redacted] Rivera & [redacted]
15727 Tetley St
Unit 5C
Hacienda Heights, CA 91745

Dear Officer,

I am writing this letter in support of my brother, [redacted] and his wife [redacted] Rivera who has recently applied for an adjustment in status.
I met [redacted] personally a few years ago when my wife and I came to visit [redacted] and [redacted] in California.

[redacted] was very gracious and friendly and it was a pleasure meeting both her and her parents.
In the time that they have been together, it has become obvious that [redacted] is very good for my brother [redacted] and my entire family has come to think of [redacted] as one of us.
We not only fully support [redacted] desire for citizenship, we are very much looking forward to seeing her again when she gains citizenship and is able to travel to see us.

I know that she would be a valuably and productive citizen if given the opportunity.

Please contact me if you need any further information.

Sincerely,

Laurie Jerome
5198 State Highway 12
Norwich, NY 13815
United States Citizen

May 10, 2018

Re: [redacted]
15727 Tetley St.
Unit 5C
Hacienda Heights, CA 91745

Dear Officer,

I write this to attest to the character of my sister-in-law [redacted] Q. [redacted] who is married legally to my brother, [redacted] is a hard-working, honest woman who has proven herself to be very good to my brother and to everyone she meets. She is pleasant and good-hearted, and a very much-loved member of our family, I truly hope you will carefully consider her application for citizenship.

If you have questions or need for further information, please contact me by phone (607-371-1474) or by mail at the above address.

Best regards,

Laurie Jerome

Christie Walker

1707 Airport Rd.

Moneta, VA 24121

4/14/18

Re: [redacted] Rivera & [redacted] [redacted]

15727 Tedley St.

Unit 5C

Hacienda Heights, CA 91745

Dear Officer,

I am writing this on behalf of my brother and his wife who has applied for Adjustment of Status.

I, Christie Walker, and my husband John Walker have been very happy to welcome [redacted] into our family for the past 8 years. She has been a caring and loving wife to my brother. She has been kind and thoughtful to everyone in our large family, reaching out to everyone with her giving spirit. She is hard working, keeps her home immaculate, and is always sharing her wonderful cooking with her neighbors.

[redacted] needs to be here with her family and friends. She is honest, dependable and an asset to any community, certainly to our family. [redacted] has been waiting so very long for this, she has completed all her obligations and deserves to be here where she belongs.

I thank you in advance for taking our thoughts and wishes into consideration in this matter. Feel free to contact me if you need anything further.

Sincerely,

Wendy L. Slavin
US Citizen Born 12/16/1952
360 Lafayette St.
Hackettstown, NJ 07840
201-230-9654

May 17, 2018

Re: [redacted] and [redacted]
15727 Tetley St. Unit 5C
Hacienda Heights, CA 91745

Dear Officer,

I'm writing in support of my sister in law, [redacted] and also in regard to her marriage to my brother [redacted]

I have known [redacted] for eight years now, and have seen her with [redacted] my family, and with hers. [redacted] is an honest and responsible individual with a good conscience, and a warm and caring heart. She is an intelligent and talented person, who certainly helps to make the world a better place.

Her marriage to [redacted] is an inspiration to us all, as their love and respect for each other is as strong and loving today as it was in the beginning of their relationship. We love her and are glad and proud to have her as a member of our family.

This is what I know to be accurate and true, and hope that it will help you in your consideration of [redacted] application. Please reach out to me with any questions or concerns.

Sincerely,

Wendy L. Slavin

Wendy L. Slavin

Clarita G. Rivera
1821 Camino Viejo Apt. C
Rowland Heights, CA 91748
(626) 466 6245
US Citizen

April 27, 2018

Re: [redacted] G. [redacted] and [redacted] G. [redacted]
15727 Tetley St. Unit 5C
Hacienda Heights, CA 91745

Dear Officer,

I am writing this letter on behalf of my daughter [redacted] G. [redacted] and her husband [redacted] G. [redacted]

It is both a blessing and a gift knowing that my daughter is fortunate and blessed to be married to [redacted] who is very loving, caring and thoughtful husband to my daughter for eight and half years now. All of us in the family are very happy and appreciative of [redacted] very caring and helpful ways. Me and my husband, Ernesto are very thankful that he has become part of our family.

My daughter and son-in-law are very loving, caring and respectful of me and my husband. Being senior citizens now, they never hesitate and are always there to help us. Whenever there is an emergency in the family they drive me and my husband to our doctor's appointments and other errands whenever my husband is not able to drive.

With this being said, their love, concern and support and very loving ways has been given not only to us parents but to other family members as well.

We wish and pray for many happy years for this beautiful couple.

Please do not hesitate to contact me if you need more information.

Very sincerely yours,

Clarita G. Rivera

Ernesto P. Rivera
1821 Camino Viejo Apt. C
Rowland Heights, CA 91748
(626) 383 5930
US Citizen

April 27, 2018

Re: [redacted] G. [redacted] and [redacted] G. [redacted]
15727 Tetley St. Unit 5C
Hacienda Heights, CA 91745

Dear Officer,

It is a pleasure and an honor to write this letter for my daughter [redacted] G. Rivera and my son-in-law [redacted] G. [redacted]. It has been a blessing to have [redacted] as our son-in-law.

Through the years me and my wife and the whole family have grown to love and be fond of our son-in-law. He has shown us how loving, very caring and respectful he is not only to our daughter but to us and the whole family.

Whenever the need arises that me and my wife needed help [redacted] and [redacted] are always there for us to help, guide and assist. I remember sometime in 2011 when I had a health problem and I was hospitalized. They would frequently visit us and drive my wife and bring us food and constantly checks on us if we are doing okay.

It is a great gift and a big blessing knowing that my youngest daughter is married to a very loving, responsible and caring man. As a father, I am very thankful and blessed to know that my youngest daughter is in good hands and happily married to a fine gentleman.

Each Christmas and other Holidays have become happier and memorable for me and my wife with them always there to share their loving, caring, thoughtful and generous ways.

Please contact me if you need more information about my daughter and son-in-law.

Very respectfully yours,

Ernesto P. Rivera

Exhibit '10'

Photos of the Beneficiary and the Petitioner showing Relationship

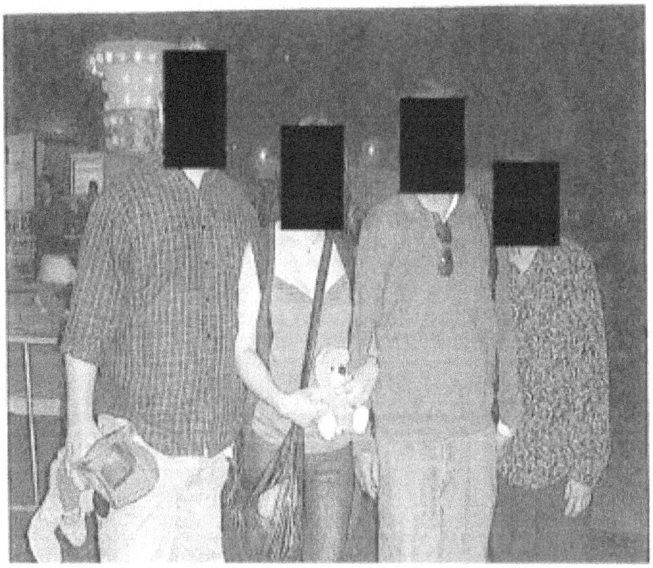

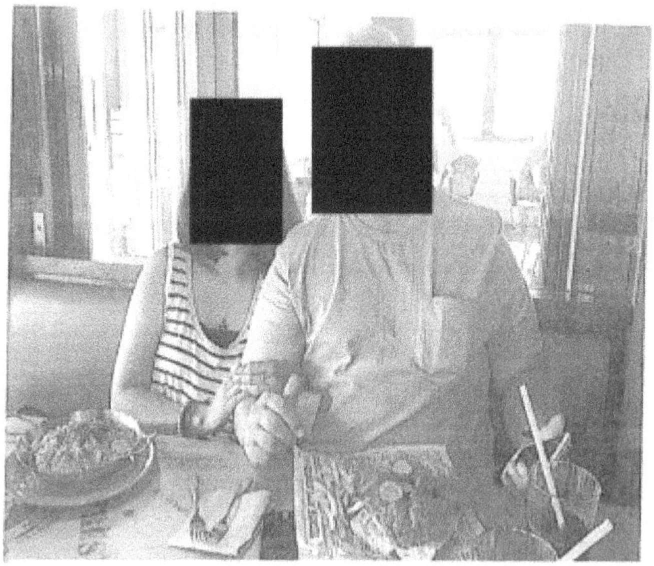

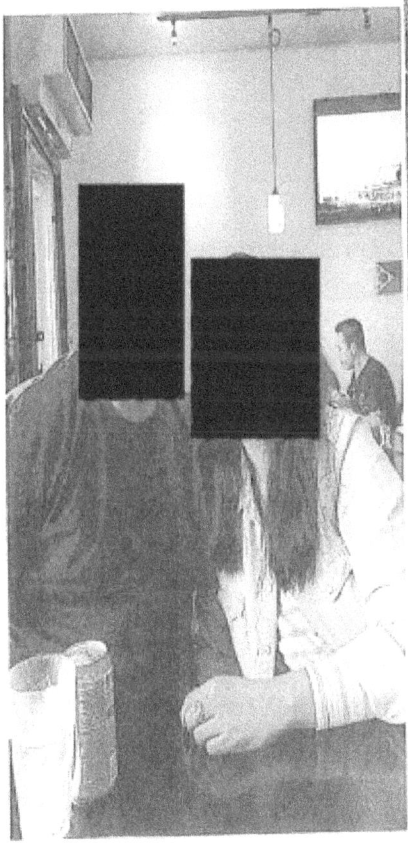

| PAGE

ABOUT THE AUTHOR

BRIAN D. LERNER IS an Immigration Lawyer and runs a National Immigration Law Firm for nearly 30 years. He is an attorney who is a certified specialist that might help in Immigration & Nationality Law as issued by the California State Bar, Board of Legal Specialization. Attorney Lerner is an expert in Immigration Law, Removal and Deportation, Citizenship, Waiver and Appeals.

He has been a licensed attorney since 1992 and started the Law Offices of Brian D. Lerner, APC. The immigration practice consists of Immigration and Nationality Law, and everything involved with and regarding immigration which includes citizenship, investment visas, family and employment visas, removal and deportation hearings, appeals, waivers, adjustment, consulate processing and all types of immigration and citizenship matters.

He has represented clients from all over the U.S. and in many countries around the world. One side of his practice is dedicated to keeping people in the U.S. and fighting for their immigration rights, while another side is to get people back who have been deported and removed from the U.S.

Also, there is the affirmative part of Immigration Law which Brian Lerner has helped numerous people come into the U.S. on business visas, investment visas, student visas, fiancée and marriage visas, religious visas and many more. Attorney Lerner has helped immigrants who are victims of crime and domestic violence or ones that are married to abusers.

In other words, Attorney Lerner has a firm that helps people all over the U.S. He has dedicated significant time to preparing numerous petitions and applications for you to get at a fraction of the price of hiring an attorney. He says it is the next best thing to a real attorney because they are real petitions prepared by an expert.

www.ingramcontent.com/pod-product-compliance
Ingram Content Group UK Ltd.
Pitfield, Milton Keynes, MK11 3LW, UK
UKHW051118290926
15471UKWH00010B/1753

9 781948 774956